ON YOUR OWN
as a YOUNG ADULT
FACILITATOR'S GUIDE

Self-Advocacy Case Studies

Betsy Krebs
Paul Pitcoff

On Your Own as a Young Adult Facilitator's Guide

© 2006 by Betsy Krebs and Paul Pitcoff
Published by JIST Life, an imprint of JIST Publishing, Inc.
8902 Otis Avenue
Indianapolis, IN 46216-1033
Phone: 1-800-648-JIST   Fax: 1-800-JIST-FAX
E-mail: info@jist.com   Web site: www.jist.com

Note to Instructors

This *Facilitator's Guide* accompanies the student book *On Your Own as a Young Adult: Self-Advocacy Case Studies* (1-55864-164-5).

Also available is the video *On Your Own as a Young Adult* (DVD 1-55864-167-X and VHS 1-55864-166-1).

Visit www.jist.com for information on JIST, free job search information, book excerpts, and ordering information on our many products! For free information on 14,000 job titles, visit www.careeroink.com.

Quantity discounts are available for JIST books. Please call our Sales Department at 1-800-648-5478 for a free catalog and more information.

Acquisitions Editors: Barb Terry and Randy Haubner
Development Editor: Jill Mazurczyk
Cover Designer: designLab
Interior Designer: Aleata Howard
Interior Layout: Marie Kristine Parial-Leonardo
Proofreader: Jeanne Clark

Printed in the United States of America
10 09 08 07 06 05   9 8 7 6 5 4 3 2 1

We have been careful to provide accurate information in this book, but it is possible that errors and omissions have been introduced. Please consider this in making any career plans or other important decisions. Trust your own judgment above all else and in all things.

Trademarks: All brand names and product names used in this book are trade names, service marks, trademarks, or registered trademarks of their respective owners.

ISBN 1-55864-165-3

About This Book

On Your Own as a Young Adult Facilitator's Guide is a *guide* for the facilitator rather than a script or a prescribed approach to using *On Your Own as a Young Adult: Self-Advocacy Case Studies*. This *Facilitator's Guide* relies on the Socratic Method to teach self-advocacy. The Socratic Method encourages critical thinking by giving student questions, not answers. Continually asking questions leads students to their own logical conclusions. Students will analyze 22 real-life case studies that they can apply to their own lives. They will explore these important skills to help them take control of their lives:

- How to plan and reach goals
- How systems and organizations work
- How your strengths are important
- How to make transitions
- How to find mentors and allies
- How to depersonalize issues
- How to recognize the needs of others
- How to use rules, laws, and rights
- How to make a self-advocacy presentation

Table of Contents

Supplemental Material

The following appendices are located at www.jist.com/K1653/Appendices.pdf.

Appendix D: **Pre-evaluation**

Appendix E: **Model Answers for Pre-evaluation**

Appendix F: **Final Evaluation**

Appendix G: **Model Answers for Final Evaluation**

Appendix H: **Professional's Feedback Form for the Informational Interview**

Appendix I: **Student Feedback Form for the Informational Interview**

Appendix J: **Midterm Report to Parent or Guardian**

Appendix K: **Model Recommendation Letter**

Appendix L: **Model Certificate of Completion**

Introduction

Overview of the Seminar

The *Getting Beyond the System®: Self-Advocacy Seminar* was developed and is taught by the Youth Advocacy Center (YAC). The Seminar is currently being replicated in other sites across the country. This Seminar educates students between the ages of 16 and 21 in the practice and theory of self-advocacy. The objective of the Seminar is to help students take control of their lives by learning to establish individual long-term career goals and to make plans to reach their goals using self-advocacy. Three products have been developed to teach this Seminar: *On Your Own as a Young Adult: Self-Advocacy Case Studies*, *On Your Own as a Young Adult Facilitator's Guide*, and *On Your Own as a Young Adult* video. The objective of these products is to extend the reach of the Seminar to other settings and to other parts of the country.

Many students will be facing independence with limited support or, in some cases, without any support. For most of the students, self-advocacy is an essential skill they have not yet developed. Therefore, it is of paramount importance that students learn how to engage the support of others in the pursuit of their individual goals.

Self-advocacy is a methodology for obtaining support from others. All successful people need self-advocacy to move toward their goals and overcome challenges in their lives. Some people pick up this skill without any formal training.

Self-advocacy requires that an individual understands the needs and goals of others, presents a positive image of him- or herself, and develops solutions that will provide mutual benefits. Unfortunately, many students have developed the antithesis of these skills: Rather than present their considerable range of positive attributes, they present problems; rather than understand the needs and goals of others, they focus exclusively on their own needs; rather than developing mutually beneficial solutions, they personalize anyone's resistance to helping them.

Self-advocacy skills are critical for achieving personal and career goals. Most successful people learn self-advocacy skills naturally in their home environment. Young adults from disadvantaged backgrounds have fewer opportunities to learn good self-advocacy skills. In some cases, their experiences create negative advocacy skills. For example, acting out gets attention. This Seminar is designed to help young adults learn and practice self-advocacy skills to take control of their lives and gain support in achieving their goals.

The Seminar consists of 12 weekly classes that each meet for 2½ hours. There are two major goals of the Seminar:

- To master skills and understanding of self-advocacy

- To prepare for a future career goal

The methodology for the Seminar is based on the Socratic Case Method traditionally used in most law schools and by a growing number of progressive educators at all levels. The cases from *On Your Own as a Young Adult: Self-Advocacy Case Studies* provide the material for learning the process of self-advocacy. Students learn to analyze situations calling for self-advocacy and formulate self-advocacy approaches.

The final project for the Seminar is conducting the informational interview, analyzing the process, and making a follow-up plan based on the results of the interview. Preparing for and conducting an informational interview is the method used to launch the process of preparing for a future career goal.

A student's progress is evaluated through the results of a final exam, homework grades, feedback from the informational interviewer, and class participation.

Seminar Topics

The Seminar educates students in the fundamentals of self-advocacy. It stresses important subjects such as

- Planning for and Reaching Your Goals
- Understanding How Systems and Organizations Work
- The Importance of Presenting Your Strengths
- Understanding the Process of Transitions
- Finding and Using Mentors and Allies
- Depersonalizing Issues and Recognizing the Needs of Others
- Developing and communicating workable solutions
- Making Self-Advocacy Presentations
- Understanding and Using Rules, Laws, and Rights
- Conducting an Informational Interview

These topics are studied using the Socratic Case Method. Students engage in cases carefully designed to create an understanding of self-advocacy concepts and to relate to students' lives.

Students and the facilitator use each class to discuss assigned cases from *On Your Own as a Young Adult: Self-Advocacy Case Studies,* answer questions about the cases, and discuss planning for their informational interviews.

Informational Interview

The culminating project for students to apply their newly acquired self-advocacy skills is the informational interview. Each student is asked to select a career in which he or she is interested. This is the individual's decision. On the basis of this decision, an expert in the chosen career field is asked to give the student a 30-minute informational interview at the interviewer's place of work.

For students, the purpose of these interviews is to gain valuable information about their career choices and advice about how to reach their career objectives. Each student is completely on his or her own in this interview. The combination of the student's self-advocacy skills and the receptiveness of the expert determine the relative success and value of the interview. Students respond positively to this challenge since the objective is highly relevant to their needs.

The informational interview as a final project is a useful way of reviewing and applying all the topics studied throughout the semester. The students understand that their ability to advocate for themselves will, in many ways, determine the success of the interview. Most students consider the interview highly important and are motivated to do their best at reviewing and applying their self-advocacy skills.

Following is an excerpt from the video, *On Your Own as a Young Adult,* available separately.

Sashine

Eighteen-year-old Sashine loved art and wanted to be a graphic designer. Placed in temporary foster homes, she coped with an ever-changing roster of caseworkers, social workers, therapists, lawyers, and judges focused on her troubled family life and on past and present crises. Terrified about making the transition out of foster care, yet knowing that she wanted to take control of her life, Sashine enrolled in the Getting Beyond the System: Self-Advocacy Seminar. She labored to learn self-advocacy, conducted an informational interview with a professional graphic artist, and used her new skills and support to enroll in the Parsons School of Design.

Sashine's desire for success and her experience of feeling trapped in the child welfare system is typical. It is stories like Sashine's, with the collision of two worlds—young adults with dreams and potential and the larger community that can offer them a chance at a successful future—that have haunted us and motivated us to create this self-advocacy education program.

Many students in your Seminar will have never met or talked with a professional outside the fields of education, mental health, or law. Many young adults lack understanding of what it takes to become an adult. Empowering students requires equipping them to successfully engage professionals who are not obligated to provide them with specific assistance. Your students will initially be resistant to and uninformed of the nature and purpose of the informational interview. Preparing them for this experience and providing an opportunity to independently conduct an informational interview will profoundly enhance their sense of strength and independence and facilitate the empowerment process.

How to Use the Facilitator's Guide

The success of the Seminar requires the combination of three essential elements. Central to the success is the creativity and experience you bring to the Seminar, the efforts of the students to actively engage in the process, and using the syllabus and lesson plans provided in this *Facilitator's Guide.* The lesson plans as tools can be extremely useful, but they have little value without the creative engagement of the facilitator and students.

You are encouraged to do your own preparation and lead discussions in the style and manner you feel is most effective. The outlines presented are only a means to begin your own thinking about how to handle each case. Do not feel compelled to rigidly follow the lesson plans.

For each case, the *Facilitator's Guide* provides some background to help develop an approach to the case, some ideas for discussion, and in some cases, a model of specific understandings we think would be useful for the students to evaluate.

"Correct answers" are not supplied because the purpose is to develop understanding by encouraging analysis. There are numerous correct answers for each question. In some cases, your students will discover new "correct answers" we have not discovered ourselves.

All of us who have worked with or parented young adults recognize that in practice it is very difficult to tell them what to do. The case studies are designed to help young adults develop understanding about the adult and work worlds and begin the process of career preparation. This Seminar offers students an understanding of the process in a neutral manner and relies on their own unique life experiences and capacities to make their own decisions on paths they want to pursue. The Socratic Method used in the text is designed to help you achieve this goal and hold back on providing the direct advice that will either be resisted or may be irrelevant to a particular individual. By providing tools to achieve independent goals, rather than advice on what paths to pursue, you respect the students' independence and demonstrate high expectations for their capacities.

Through studying and discussing the cases in the text along with debating the answers, students will sharpen their intellectual abilities and learn more about the adult and work worlds. The cases are designed and tested for relevance to the lives and interests of the students. The students will gain more insight into themselves as they analyze and debate how characters, not too dissimilar from themselves, resolve life and work challenges. The curriculum is designed to help students develop understanding and tools to make their transitions to adulthood successful.

Usually a Seminar session will consist of some general discussion about the major topic, discussion about the case given for homework, discussions about cases given in class, and when time permits, some role-playing of hypothetical situations or of the informational interview. The class will usually end with an introduction to the home-work assignment for the next class and an update on how to continue preparing for the informational interview.

When working on cases in class, it may be useful to break the class into groups to encourage collaboration. This way, each group can read and discuss the case in preparation to making a presentation to the entire class.

You may want to focus the first part of the discussion on "briefing the case." This focuses the students on the first two general questions following the case. Thus, students must first identify key facts in the case, such as goals and strengths of the protagonist, needs of the other party, outstanding issues, etc.

Recruitment and Orientation
Recruitment

Recruiting is an important aspect of conducting a successful Seminar. Students should not be expected to appreciate the value of the Seminar from just a causal description. The Seminar is a significant commitment of time and concentration, and you need to educate students about its value. Having an orientation session provides this opportunity.

When speaking with youth, it is important to remember that they all have the potential to benefit from the Seminar regardless of their present academic standing or performance in other programs. An interest in a successful future is the critical admissions requirement for this Seminar.

Recruitment must take place at multiple levels of the organization. Reinforcement from multiple sources in the organization will stimulate a prospective student to think about the opportunity in different ways. The more staff members you inform about the Seminar and include in recruiting students, the more successful you will be in interesting students.

Engaging staff to talk individually with likely candidates is the most effective manner of recruitment. Engaging Seminar graduates to recruit is equally effective in creating interest. In designing your approaches, understanding of the particular motivations of your students will help you shape a presentation that will be well-attended. YAC has used the following themes:

- Are you interested in your future?

- Do you want to reach your future career goals?

- Would you like to meet with a top professional in your chosen career field to learn how to reach your goals?

- Do you want more control of your life?

- Are you up for a challenge?

- Are you interested in a college-level experience?

If you know a student's present career goal, talk directly about that goal and discuss how the Seminar will help teach the student self-advocacy and send him or her on an informational interview.

Orientation

After you get your staff on board and plan the student outreach, you should plan and carry out a Seminar orientation session one or two weeks before the first class begins. Give enough time for staff to get the word out, yet do not allow too much time to pass or the youth will lose interest. Staff should continually remind students. Flyers providing information about the date, time, and location of the orientation should be distributed to prospective students. Empowering messages on the flyers are most likely to engage youth.

The orientation session should be run in a similar manner as you would lead the actual classes. Use the Socratic Method from the very beginning to demonstrate that there will be more discussion than lecture in the Seminar. Use the Orientation session to focus attention on the students' future and your respect for their ability to determine their own goals.

Present the informational interview as a means to excite students about the prospect of beginning their career planning. Initially, it is the part of the Seminar that is most interesting and best understood. Ask potential students what they dream about and give them the freedom to dream. Never dismiss a student's career choice, no matter how unlikely or ridiculous it seems, as this will turn them off immediately. Ask potential students if they have ever met anyone that works in that field and ask them if they would like to meet someone that does. Tell them you will introduce them to that person if they complete the Seminar. Show the video *On Your Own as a Young Adult* (available separately) to lead a conversation about the video and informational interviews. Appendix C in this *Facilitator's Guide* is a group of discussion questions pertaining to the video.

Graduation also encourages youth to attend the Seminar. Tell potential students at the orientation that they will receive a certificate of achievement at a ceremony when they complete the Seminar. Many students are thrilled with achieving something that concludes with a formal celebration, advancing their self-respect. Potential students should also know that they can put the Seminar on their résumés and receive a letter of recommendation from their facilitator.

Collect information from students who want to sign up for the first class. The YAC uses an application to gauge their motivation and commitment to future goals. Appendix A of this *Facilitator's Guide* contains a sample application. To reinforce the seriousness and to continue interest until the first class, we usually give out the first homework assignment, Case #1. This also provides a common experience to discuss immediately on the first day of class.

We suggest that the orientation be held on the same time and day of the week as the scheduled Seminar meetings. This will hopefully lead to less scheduling conflicts. It may also be worth your time to e-mail or call students who attend the Seminar prior to the first class or ask the people who referred them to remind them of the first class.

Admissions to the Self-Advocacy Seminar

The Seminar is designed to work for students at many different academic levels. The common and most important requirement for success in the Seminar is **motivation.** We have seen students with weak academic skills achieve great results in the Seminar and demonstrate academic skills above their performance at school.

Admission into the Seminar is based on judging the motivation and commitment of the young person to engage in the challenging work until the end of the semester. You may want to require that interested students formally apply. (A sample application is available in Appendix A of this *Facilitator's Guide*.) In their applications, candidates should explain why they want to take the Seminar and indicate some long-term future goals. Past academic performance should not be an element in the selection process.

After a student's application is accepted, it may be useful to give the student a contract to communicate the seriousness of the Seminar. (A sample contract is available in Appendix B of this *Facilitator's Guide*.) The contract states what the student will learn and what commitment they must make to learn self-advocacy skills and conduct an informational interview. It's a good idea to go over the contract with the students as another way of communicating the nature of the Seminar.

Expectations

Expectations play a large role in shaping the future of a young person. When faced with the dismal statistics of failure for young adults from disadvantaged backgrounds, it is natural for your expectations to be lowered. In an effort to be caring, one often lowers expectations for young adults to "save them from disappointment." You may also become overwhelmed with their educational deficits and the negative environments they have encountered. In spite of these factors, it is important to maintain high expectations for all of your students.

You are teaching this Seminar because you believe your students have the potential to achieve success both in the class and in their future. High expectations are a powerful factor in reversing the failure rate for young adults heading toward independence. If you repeatedly express your high expectations, you will also help students become engaged in the learning process.

In the Seminar, your students have one overriding identity, and that is their future goal. Chantel will be a pastry chef, Benny will be a sociologist, Omar will be a graphic artist, and Shermane will be a sonogram technologist. Their past is important only in the strengths it has provided for them. Their present problems are put aside for the Seminar so they can begin the work of creating their future. Your job is to take their ambition seriously because it will give them strength to succeed. Your role is to help each student learn the process of self-advocacy. If successful, this process will lead them to either adjust their preparation for their goals or develop different goals. At this moment, learning the process is more important than selecting the "right" career goal.

In the first few weeks, students are adjusting to the entire scope of the Seminar. Confusion and frustration are to be expected from students in this new situation and the work demanded from them. You must continuously reinforce that this confusion and frustration is normal.

Eventually, you may begin to see many positive responses to the Seminar and the work. Be patient. Some of the breakthroughs students make as a direct result of your teaching may not occur until after the Seminar is completed. Some may not occur for years. As a facilitator, you need to recognize this phenomenon and not expect to have immediate feedback from all students.

Students must be required to engage in the written homework assignments. At first students may do very poorly in their comprehension of the case and questions and their ability to express themselves in writing. Some students may not complete all of the homework. As poor as their performances may be, you need to reinforce any achievement they make. Use any kernel of written achievement as a way to engage them to work more diligently on future homework. In your feedback, relate to the issues rather than their flawed command of language. (See Appendix B of the student's casebook for an example.)

Future Identity and Strengths

In this Seminar, the students' identities are focused on their strengths and their futures. In every interchange, try to refer to and integrate the students' future goals. Remember their strengths and try to refer to these strengths in making class illustrations. If you have a visitor in the class, make sure that you or the student makes introductions that include the student's future goal. For example, say, "I would like you to meet Antoine, he is going to be an animator. He's also a very good storyteller."

If you have time, try to cut out articles or identify Web sites that relate to each of the students' identified career goals. Even if you cannot do it for all the students, demonstrate the process of researching a career based on the goals of one or two students in your Seminar. Find actual job postings that demonstrate the variety of opportunities in that field. Select students you know are particularly insecure and intimidated by pursuing such research. For the careers selected, show how to look at newspapers, magazines, etc. and pick out any articles that relate to future goals. Finally, encourage all Seminar students to be on the lookout for information about careers of any of their fellow students.

The following are techniques we have successfully used to elevate a student's identity with his or her future.

Initial Identification with the Future

During initial contact in recruitment or before the Seminar begins, you can help students identify future goals:

- Ask about their future career goals.

- Question in an open and accepting way.

- Treat them as future professionals who are developing expertise in their field.

- Avoid being judgmental about a career field even if you think it's crazy, such as brain surgery, tight end of the Jets, NBC anchorperson, etc.

- Take their ambitions seriously; write them down.

- Students are used to reports relating to their past problems, health situations, deficiencies, etc. Make a big deal about their "future folder," which contains only constructive things.

- Help students be more specific or identify what more they need to know.

- Bring up the issue of backup plans. Don't worry if they don't respond to this now.

Adopting the Future Identity

After students have selected identities, help them adopt these identities.

- Reference should be made in almost every class for each student.

- Introduce students to others by their future identify, such as, "Jasmine is going to be a computer programmer…," "Benny is going to be a nuclear health technician…," etc. As the semester progresses, try to make the identities more specific.

- When illustrating points connected to classwork, relate to a student's future identity. For example, "The character in the case has an interesting problem. Benny, your job will also depend upon you working a specific schedule. How would you suggest the character in the case negotiate a change in his schedule?"

- Bring in clippings or stories of professionals in the fields your students have chosen to strive toward.

- Refer back to your own personal journey of going from ignorance about your career field to your current professional success. Share these stories with the students.

- Try to keep the context of your discussions connected to future goals of students. For example, if you want to teach importance of savings or how to find an apartment, you could use the following example:

"Jasmine is working as a computer programmer trainee. It is her first job out of college. She doesn't make a lot of money and owes some money for her education. How should she approach finding an apartment or saving money?" Keep referring to Jasmine's future goal while continuing to discuss her need to save.

These little reminders make students feel that their goals must be serious because others are taking them seriously.

On Your Own as a Young Adult: Self-Advocacy Case Studies

On Your Own as a Young Adult: Self-Advocacy Case Studies is the complete text for the Seminar. The text, the facilitator's questions, and the student analysis are the core learning sources for the Seminar.

The text breaks down the process of self-advocacy into chapters based on the many skills required to be a self-advocate. Each chapter begins with an explanation of the concepts and is followed by "cases" for the students to analyze. The cases mostly focus on central characters that have had significant adversity in their early lives. These characters encounter challenges that must be resolved using self-advocacy skills.

Case analysis sharpens the critical-thinking ability of the students. Focusing on gathering facts, analyzing their meaning, understanding the issues presented, and developing approaches to solutions gives students a wider vision of challenges they will face in their own lives.

Students find the cases relevant because they relate to characters that have had significant early life hardships and present situations the students will soon encounter. The cases derive from stories of real people. Informing students of this fact helps to reinforce the relevancy of the cases to their own lives. Using the stories of other people defuses defensiveness and makes it easier for students to make critical analyses.

Each case is followed by questions. Usually questions 1 and 2 are general to all cases. They help a student *brief a case:* identify facts and issues and develop solutions. A model of a briefed case is in Appendix B of *On Your Own as a Young Adult: Self-Advocacy Case Studies.* Students need to work on briefing a case to develop their abilities to identify and analyze facts and issues in any situation.

The remaining questions directly relate to the subject of the case and help the students learn various concepts. Read through the questions and assign either all or some questions, depending upon your assessment of the needs of the students and their mastery of the material they need to learn.

The cases range in complexity and use differing approaches to the presentation. Some cases develop specific challenges for the protagonist and others are used solely for the analysis of the underlining self-advocacy dynamics. These differences help to maintain student and facilitator interest as well as provide an expansive approach to self-advocacy analysis.

A couple cases are repeated with a different emphasis in the questions. This gives students an opportunity to study these cases in-depth and recognize the differing analyses and principles that can emerge from the same facts.

Conducting the Seminar
Using the Socratic Case Method

Intellectual empowerment is an important goal of the Seminar. In our society, no individual will succeed without the ability to utilize his or her intellectual potential. Consequently, the Seminar's methodology has equal importance with its content.

The Seminar is based on the premise that students have strong intellectual potential. In many cases, this potential has not been tapped. Your students have rarely enjoyed the intellectual challenge and heightened learning produced by the Socratic Case Method.

Rather than having students memorize the methods and theory of self-advocacy, the Seminar focuses on learning to think like a self-advocate. Rather than impart particular knowledge, the method develops understanding. It helps both students and facilitator understand issues, analyze advocacy problems, reason by analogy, and think critically about their own approach and the approach of others. Through understanding, students can apply knowledge and skills to match their individual needs and capabilities.

The Socratic Case Method requires and supports a facilitator's ability to learn in the process. As a result, the Seminar can attract facilitators who have a high level of intellectual ability and accomplishments. Whether teaching a case for the first time or the tenth time, the Socratic Case Method always produces new visions, new insights, and new understandings of self-advocacy dynamics.

The Seminar focuses on giving students questions rather than answers. Many students find this process different and difficult. They sometimes resist the process because of the difficulty and the tension created by not getting finite answers. It is important not to take their resistance personally. The curriculum and approach have worked with many students.

The Socratic Method requires the facilitator to ask many open-ended questions that will stimulate the students to analyze the cases with more thought. Some facilitators use evidence-type questions that require students to clarify an answer. These question ask students

- To give an example that demonstrates their response to a question

- To explain why they think they are right

- To explain what would convince them to have a different answer

- To use specific facts from the case to support their analysis

Many students want to be asked questions. This is an important opportunity for them to formulate their own ideas and hear their ideas expressed to an audience. Through verbalizing their thinking, they gain increased knowledge of the **process** of analysis, self-advocacy, and planning for their futures. Even students who are not assertive in class often value the opportunity to express their thinking.

Your challenge is to encourage the students to **think.** Guide them. Resist giving answers. Give them ideas. When possible, respond to the discussion by asking more questions: "What do you think?" or "What would you do?" or "What's the reason for your answer?"

The classic Socratic Method views the facilitator as the "questioner" rather than teacher or leader. In this type of relationship, the questioner is equal in understanding with the "respondent" (student). Neither the questioner nor the respondent has *the* correct answer. The hierarchy dynamics in the classroom are diminished. With the Socratic Case Method, students become empowered to think on their own and accept understanding through their own intellectual process rather than have it imparted from authority. This change in dynamics from a traditional classroom can be unsettling for both facilitator and student but, if adopted, will greatly improve the preparation for successful independence.

Incorporating the Socratic Method transfers much responsibility for learning to the student. The Socratic Method relies on a theory of education that concludes that students develop understanding of new topics through analysis and refuting of their reasoning. It is not your job to supply the "correct" answer to your students. In practice, this is very difficult to implement because you will often have good ideas of what would be the best answer to a question or the best solution for one of the protagonists in the cases.

In addition, many of us hold to a model of education where the teacher supplies answers to the student. Therefore, it is important to work extremely hard to refrain from giving your students answers to the questions posed in the cases or answers to questions you yourself ask. Rather, work at developing additional questions as a way of refuting inadequate student answers and to help students strengthen their analytic ability until they gain sufficient understanding of the topics presented.

Class Participation

Following are techniques to promote the Socratic Method and student discussion:

- Encourage students to learn each other's names, career goals, and individual strengths.

- Arrange seating to promote discussion. Students will more readily talk to someone opposite them than next to them; thus, semi-circles or circles are useful. Do not allow students to sit isolated from the group.

- Attempt to bring out learning points through student comments and limit your own lecturing. The artistry of the Socratic Case Method is to stimulate students to discuss the process of self-advocacy for themselves.

- It is especially important to give each student an opportunity to talk during the first two classes. This will make it easier to get full participation in later classes.

- Divide students into small groups to work on some cases. This allows students to express ideas with each other. Go to each group and stimulate their discussion. Appoint a member for each group to report back to the full class.

- Quiet students should be encouraged to participate.

    - Small groups are effective.

    - Begin with casual questions that require little detail.

- Give rewards to quiet students: Repeat their ideas and refer to these ideas later in the class. For example, write "Jasmine's theory" and her comments on the board.

- Stand or sit close to a quiet student.

- Limit students who monopolize the discussion.

    - Small groups are effective.

    - Limit eye contact with "monopolizer."

    - Ask everyone to jot down an answer and call on the quieter students.

There are no wrong answers in class. Try to find some element in each answer that has merit and focus on that aspect of the answer.

The classes must have a positive and supportive atmosphere. Students must feel safe to experiment with different techniques, explore their own strengths, and make mistakes.

Storytelling

An important learning experience for children growing up is listening to stories. Before a child goes out into the world, he or she learns about it through listening to stories. Most of your students have not heard many stories from adults. Your students will greatly value any personal stories you tell about experiences in which you have used self-advocacy or struggled with some challenge. They need both the information inherent in the story and the model of someone successfully achieving personal goals.

If you tell personal stories, you will also bridge much of the gap that intimidates students and creates suspicion because of the differences between your age and experiences and theirs.

Students are particularly responsive to stories in which you demonstrate some mistake or screw-up and how you overcame it. This proves to them that no one is perfect and success is achieved through a path of mistakes and failures as well as hard work and acquiring new knowledge and skills.

If you are willing to tell such personal stories, ensure that students understand you are not giving them a prescription for exactly how to proceed with a certain type of challenge.

Informational Interview

The *informational interview* is the focal point for the semester's work. In this interview, students gain an opportunity to practice the self-advocacy skills they learned during the semester. They also have the opportunity to gain valuable information about their intended career field and the methods for reaching their goals in the field. The successful student finds these informational interviews a significant milestone in his or her path to achieving future goals.

By the third week in the semester, students should give you a written description of the career field they are interested in pursuing. During the middle of the semester, you or your organization should find an experienced professional in the career field selected by each student in the Seminar. While these experts usually have no prior contact with the program, they usually are willing to commit to a thirty-minute interview to help a student plan their future. Typically, those willing to do the interviews spend more time with the student and become involved in the process of providing advice and, in some cases, future resources. Some experts have spent up to two hours with students and offered valuable internships.

An important dynamic of the informational interview process derives from the fact that students recognize that their expert interviewee has no prior commitment to them. It is completely up to the student to engage the professional and gain his or her interest. Many students become anxious about the interview because it may be the first time they meet with an experienced professional in their field of interest. The anxiety comes from recognizing that this is an important interview and its success depends solely upon their skills.

Preparing for independence requires that students take responsibility for important initiatives in their lives. This informational interview is very important to most students, and therefore, they must take a good deal of responsibility in preparing for and conducting it. Yet knowing that their self-advocacy is entirely up to them naturally makes them anxious. Believing that they could fail at something that is important creates further anxiety.

One of your tasks is to acknowledge that this anxiety is rational and experienced by most people in similar situations. You can reassure the students about the probable outcome and explain that focusing on their preparation will help to diminish their anxiety.

Very few students fail at this assignment. But ultimately, you cannot protect against failure. This is important because it places more responsibility on the student. Even if a student "messes up," he or she is doing it within your supportive environment. The consequences of an unsuccessful informational interview are not devastating. Within this environment, you can help the individual learn from any mistakes he or she makes and you can always schedule another informational interview.

The informational interview is also a catalyst toward making an ending with a present life situation and moving into the neutral zone. Using the transitions theory will help your students understand their resistance and anxiety as well as the benefits of making endings. The transitions theory will also help them appreciate the creative value of the neutral zone along with accepting this period as one of confusion and questions.

The informational interviews are conducted at the professional's office or workplace around their scheduling convenience. The interviews are private and no one other than the student and the professional and perhaps colleagues of the professional should attend. Thus, the students conduct the meeting relying completely on the skills they learned during the semester.

Ideally, students should travel to these meetings by themselves and be responsible for getting to their appointments on time and deciding their agenda and what they will wear. If you must provide transportation, do not have any accompanying staff from your organization enter the building in which the interview is conducted.

Students feel a major sense of accomplishment when the informational interview is completed. They have engaged in a discussion about their future with a professional who has already achieved success. They have great respect for this professional and therefore gain a heightened sense of confidence knowing they were able to connect with this person and get valuable and individualized advice.

The professional is asked to fill out a short feedback form that lets you and the student know what areas of his or her presentation were most successful and what areas need more work. (You can find a sample form at www.jist.com/K1653/Appendices.pdf.) Professionals will be more willing to give honest feedback if they know that negative criticism will not be directly communicated to the student. It is your job to summarize results of the informational interview based on the professional's candid feedback, the student's self-assessment, and the observation you made from their presentation to the class.

The student is also asked to fill out an evaluation form. (You can find a sample form at www.jist.com/K1653/Appendices.pdf.) Frequently, students place too much focus on the professional's personality. Students often become elated that a professional responded to them in a serious manner. This dynamic may diminish the value of the information they receive. The evaluation form helps them focus on the information they obtain as well as on their performances.

Homework

Each week students receive a homework assignment. The course syllabus indicates the due dates for specific homework and readings. This syllabus also indicates which cases will be discussed in class.

You may use all the questions given in the casebook, assign only specific questions, or include others of your own. The objective is for students to engage in the cases, analyze facts, develop strategies and possible solutions, and gain familiarity with self-advocacy.

Carefully review homework and give feedback related to each student's achievements as well as for those areas that need improvement. Give feedback that will engage the student in thinking. It is important to give homework back to students the week after it is handed in to you.

Your written feedback should give some indication of the overall performance compared to your standards. It is also important to assess students in terms of their own **relative learning process.** Breakthroughs in learning should be acknowledged even if the student's performance has not yet reached your standards.

Initially, students will be defensive and resist your written feedback. They are used to negative comments on their papers. Explain that even what appears as criticism derives from treating their work with respect. If you take the time to note and remark on positive aspects of their work, students will be more energized.

While the students' homework is a way of assessing student progress, it is not intended to judge student achievement and mastery of skills. This presents you with a challenge. While you need to give students feedback on their ability to master concepts and skills, your overall objective is to get them engaged in the learning process. Therefore, your written feedback becomes the critical element in the motivation process, rather than just indications of their performances.

In approaching a student's homework assignment, your objective is to identify examples of good fact recognition, analysis, insight, and creativity. Some students will easily display these achievements, but many will provide only limited examples. In such cases, you will need to take at least two actions:

1. Try to be open to extremely different case interpretations, and rather than focus on what is the "best answer," look to help students develop their logic for the **answer they propose.** The students will gain confidence in their thinking and you will motivate them to eventually think through their analysis to a point where they may find better answers on their own.

2. In helping students think through their answers, use the Socratic Method in your written feedback. Ask, *"What facts support your position?"* or *"What is the other party thinking?"* or *"What is the protagonist's real objective?"*

Following is an example of how to engage students who give minimal responses to homework questions.

Suppose we assigned Case #12, *Jasda Needs a Mentor*, for homework and three students answered only one question as in the example below.

Why would Ms. Greer want to be a mentor for Jasda?

Student one: *Because she likes Jasda.*

Student two: *Because she has nothing better to do.*

Student three: *She wouldn't.*

If we want to elevate expectations, we might respond as follows:

1. That's a good insight. You need to explain why she likes Jasda. This will help Jasda keep a good mentoring relationship. I think being liked is very important, but are there any other reasons Ms. Greer might want to help?

2. That's an interesting analysis I hadn't thought of. Maybe even though she is very busy, she feels she has nothing important or interesting to do. Perhaps you're getting at the point that being a mentor might be the most interesting or stimulating thing to do at this point in time. Would you suggest that Jasda then make a presentation focused on how exciting and stimulating it would be for Ms. Greer to mentor her?

3. I think you have something here. The question assumes Ms. Greer would want to be a mentor, but maybe she is just too busy or not interested. If this is true, then Jasda really has a challenge ahead of her. But when you think about it, most self-advocacy is about getting someone to do something they at first don't want to do. Because your answer is very useful, do you have any ideas how Jasda could change Ms. Greer's mind?

Look at how much we can give back to any of the students' responses. It demonstrates that their ideas are taken seriously and affect the questioner. The responses also pull the student into seriousness because, rather than trying to change their thinking, it challenges them to go further down the road they have selected.

Any student who attempts to engage in the homework and present some answers needs to be rewarded with your feedback. In addition to specific feedback for each answer, give the student some overall recognition of the progress he or she is making in some areas.

Within this context, you can suggest other areas the student is now ready to explore and work at. For example, *"You did an excellent job identifying some key facts. Now try working on analyzing how these facts affect Ben's advocacy approach,"* or *"You have a good understanding of Jasmine's long-term objectives and, therefore, are in a good position to figure out what short-term objectives to use in her plan to reach those long-term objectives,"* or *"Your understanding of the importance of identifying the other person's needs is right on the mark. You have the makings of a good self-advocate and have the potential to have a very successful informational interview."*

Students naturally want to see their overall performance measured by a grade. Students can easily be discouraged by low grades and lose some steam by high grades. Of prime importance is for students to read your feedback as well as receive their grades. They need to learn that while they can make a mistake or do poorly, there is always a route to future success.

Some students will ask if they can redo homework for a re-evaluation of their performance grade. Encourage them to do so and be willing to increase their grades.

Some students skip questions in their first homework assignments and resist the "briefing" analysis for each case. Continually explain the importance of doing all the work and urge them to complete the assignments.

Ask students to make up any missing assignments. Most students have had little structure or opportunity in their lives to commit themselves to an extended task. The weekly homework and the increasing familiarity with the "briefing" analysis will eventually feel comfortable.

Students must hand in homework for the class assigned. If they are late, it must be reflected in their grade and they must be asked not to repeat this pattern. Taking control of the future requires responding to responsibility, and completing homework is not an overly ambitious task for someone wanting a successful future.

When a student is having a particularly hard time with homework, it may be useful to ask him or her to do it over. The incentive is to master the material and increase his or her grade. Sometimes he or she will need to redo only a portion of the homework. An important inherent element in self-advocacy is learning that achieving goals requires working until successful. Students need to learn that just doing a task is different from completing it successfully. Redoing homework is one method of learning this concept.

It is very useful to model a homework assignment in class to demonstrate your standards. This will be helpful for students who have no model for the way to complete the homework.

You will note that Appendix B in the student casebook gives an example of "briefing a case." This is actually a model for completing the homework for Case #2, *Ebony's First Job Interview*. It is suggested that you don't alert students to this Appendix until after they complete the homework assignment. Later, you might refer to Appendix B for students to review and discuss in class.

Midterm Reports

By the sixth week in the Seminar, it is important to give a midterm progress letter to each student's Seminar coach (the adult that co-signed the Seminar contract.) You may use a form that communicates the nature and purpose of the Seminar and the challenges with which students must engage, as well as their general accomplishments. Use this form *and* hand-write one or two sentences after your signature that provide some specific information about the individual student's achievements in your Seminar. Focus exclusively on their positives. You can find a sample midterm report at www.jist.com/K1653/Appendices.pdf.

These midterm reports have a dramatic impact on elevating the adult's respect for the young person. When the young person gets feedback from this adult, it will contribute to his or her sense of accomplishment.

Academic Policy

Many students in your Seminar have not been held to high academic or performance standards. In many instances, it is due to lack of resources. But in some cases, these low expectations derive from a belief that the significant traumas experienced by youth from disadvantaged backgrounds will prevent them from any significant future success.

The Seminar is designed around the premise that our students have the potential to succeed, and that predictions of who will succeed cannot be made with absolute certainty. While we empathize with their traumas, past and present, we focus on the students' **future** and our ability to help them prepare for independence.

There is no reason that any student cannot succeed in the Seminar if they have the opportunity to fully engage in the work. At a minimum we urge that students

- Attend all classes

- Arrive on time

- Complete the homework

- Participate in class

- Conduct an informational interview

If they do all these things, regardless of their academic skill level, they will learn and succeed in this Seminar.

Absences from Class

Students are told they are allowed only one absence for an emergency during the entire semester. Thus, students need to be cautioned about "budgeting" this permissible absence for the most pressing emergency/conflict in their schedule. You need to reinforce this because students have experience missing activities or school without any consequences. In addition, many systems continually set up appointments for them that are cancelled at the last moment. If you allow more than one absence, the group dynamics of the Seminar will deteriorate and most students will not be able to catch up on the work. Each class is important and has critical content that cannot be duplicated.

Occasionally, a fully involved student may be forced to miss more than one class. If the student asks you to reconsider the one absence rule, you may think about this request if the student makes a good "self-advocacy" presentation that focuses on the class needs and your needs as a facilitator rather than the student's problems. This student must present a solution for how to

1. Make up the work

2. Repair the damage to the group dynamics

3. Meet your needs as the Seminar facilitator

You may have to play a dual role here. As a facilitator, you are very concerned with the second absence, the loss of momentum, the amount of work to catch up on, and the diminished potential for success with the informational interview. As the student's self-advocacy coach, you may have to step out of your facilitator role and help the student make a better presentation to you as a facilitator.

In no instance may you allow a student to miss a third class and remain in the Seminar. If a third absence happens, you need to inform the student that he or she will be unable to continue the Seminar for the remainder of the semester. This is not a punishment, and the student is welcome to reapply next semester when he or she is able to make the full commitment.

Disruptive Students

Occasionally, you may encounter a student who is so disruptive that his or her behavior prevents you or the students from moving forward with the curriculum. This student should be warned that if the behavior continues, he or she will be asked to drop the Seminar. It is not your responsibility to explore why he or she behaved in such a manner, and you should avoid being punitive. A discharged student should be told that even though he or she had some problems this semester, he or she is welcome to start again next semester.

Pre- and Final Evaluations

It is useful to give students both pre- and final evaluations. An evaluation can measure understanding of self-advocacy concepts. Sample pre- and final evaluations, as well as model answer sheets for both evaluations are available at www.jist.com/K1653/Appendices.pdf.

The pre-evaluation should be administered at the end of the first class and **should not be returned to the student because it is almost identical to the final evaluation.** Many students will not be able to answer questions on the pre-evaluation. Assure them that this is typical and explain that the purpose is to help the facilitator understand where to place emphasis during the semester. In fact, this will be a helpful guide for you.

Certificates and Letters of Recommendation

All students who successfully complete the Seminar should receive a certificate of completion and be eligible for a letter of recommendation. Your letter of recommendation should contain a description of the Seminar they completed and a paragraph about the student's particular strengths and accomplishments. You should educate students about the usefulness of the certificate and letter of recommendation in applying for internships, educational programs, and jobs. A sample certificate and letter of recommendation are available at www.jist.com/K1653/Appendices.pdf.

Roster

Facilitators should maintain a class roster that indicates

- Name and birth date of student

- Phone numbers and address of student

- Identified career goal

- Attendance

- Performance on each homework assignment

- Performance on evaluations

- Name and identification of informational interviewer

- Feedback from informational interviewer

- Notes on class participation and progress

Professional Relationship with Students

Students in your class have complex needs in terms of relationships with adults in their lives. Too often, when they feel they are in supportive relationships, the adults abruptly leave their lives. Young adults from disadvantaged backgrounds often experience separations from important adults, forced by economic and social conditions beyond anyone's control. We are cautious about supporting an expectation that we will remain in a student's life and thereby repeat the pattern of disappointment.

Students have a heightened belief that all relationships are entirely personal. Thus criticism, rejection, or even praise is considered to relate to their "likeability" rather than their performances. We believe that in the class we can help students learn how to depersonalize situations if we model a professional relationship. Thus, we should actively praise and critique their work, but make sure they understand it relates to their performance rather than their character. Our respect for the students' efforts to better their lives must always be expressed, even when they fail to succeed at a particular Seminar challenge. Our overriding respect for each student remains unconditional and expressed but does not detract from our ability to challenge his or her thinking.

Students need to learn that failure is part of the path to success and they must deal with it often. In most instances, you should not feel uncertain about holding students to high performance standards. If you can do this at the same time you convey respect for their individuality, students will eventually respond to and respect your interest in them, even when you are demanding and allow them to make mistakes.

The Seminar should be a haven for a focus on self-advocacy and future planning rather than on personal problems. However, students will attempt to engage you in their personal problems. It will be extremely difficult at first, but we discourage discussing personal problems in the Seminar context. If before or after class a student engages you in a personal issue, direct the conversation to his or her future career goal or self-advocacy or understanding of transition analysis.

If you believe the student needs immediate help, you may refer the student to the right source, but you must maintain your identity as facilitator and focus on the Seminar goals. Eventually, students will find this approach a refuge from dealing with immediate and past problems and will find comfort in an environment focused exclusively on their futures.

There will be some times when you may not be able to stop students from raising personal issues in class. If appropriate, you can allow such a discussion to run for a few minutes if you can direct it toward understanding a self-advocacy principal. For example, a student mentioning gangs in his or her neighborhood can be an opportunity for the class to discuss the importance of allies and identify the purpose and needs of the gangs.

Graduation

It is important to celebrate this ending and provide an opportunity to experience a sense of pride, accomplishment, and strength. Hopefully, this will help students learn that not all endings need to be negative and that, as in this case, the ending can create a strong launching ground for new and better experiences.

Preparing for and participating in the graduation ceremony allows students to reflect on their achievements. Learning to accept this recognition and feel worthy of it is a major ingredient to move students further toward achieving their long-term goals.

In preparing students for graduation, encourage them to bring one or more guests, listen to the speeches, and prepare to talk with some of the other invited guests. If time permits and there is a small graduating class, have each student publicly say something about his or her Seminar experience and informational interview. If there is not enough time, select one or more Seminar representatives to give a short speech about the class and informational interview.

Publicly give each student a certificate of completion and say one or two remarks about the student's strengths or accomplishments during the semester.

Seminar Syllabus
Week One

Topic: Chapter 1, "Planning for and Reaching Your Goals"

Classwork:

- Discuss the Introduction of *On Your Own*.
- Discuss "Self-Advocacy Process."
- Discuss "Methods for Briefing a Case."
- Discuss Chapter 1.
- Discuss Case #1, *Shavone's Five Career Choices*.
- Administer pre-evaluation (35 minutes).

Homework due next week:

Assigned reading:

- Review "Self-Advocacy Process."

Case homework:

- Read Case #2, *Ebony's First Job Interview.* Answer questions 1–3, 5, 7.

Informational interview homework:

- Select a career goal.

- Write two or more sentences describing the characteristics (purpose of job and what one does) of this selected career goal.

- Write two or more sentences describing why you selected this goal.

Week Two

Topic: Chapter 1, "Planning for and Reaching Your Goals" (continued)

Classwork:

- Discuss Case #2, *Ebony's First Job Interview.* Answer all questions, especially 4, 6–8.

- Discuss Case #3, *Samantha's Strategy to Change Jobs at C&E Electronics.* Answer all questions, especially 4–5.

- Discuss Case #4, *Michael Needs to Find the Facts.* Answer all questions, especially 4–7.

- Discuss Exercise #1, *Identifying Your Long- and Short-Term Goals.* Discuss and then ask students to write answers and review and edit for homework.

- Discuss the Informational interview:

  - Explain the purpose of an informational interview.

  - Discuss the importance of selecting a specific career field and the chance that such a selection may change with added information.

Homework due next week:

Assigned reading:

- Read Chapter 2, "How Systems and Organizations Work."

Case homework:

- Read Case #5, *Nat Wants to Change His Lunch Hour at Baldwin's Hardware.* Answer questions 1–7.

Informational interview homework:

- Complete Exercise #1, *Identifying Your Long- and Short-Term Goals.*

- In writing, make a final selection of a long-term career goal. (This will determine the informational interview expert.)

- Outline the information you want to get about your selected career goal and how to reach your career goal.

Week Three

Topic: Chapter 2, "How Systems and Organizations Work"

Classwork:

- Discuss Chapter 2.

- Read Exercise #2, *Jamal Finds the Missions.*

- Discuss Case #5, *Nat Wants to Change His Lunch Hour at Baldwin's Hardware.* Answer all questions, especially 8–10.

- Read Case #6, *Hipazz Asks, "Who's in Charge?"* Answer all questions, especially 5–8.

- Read Case #7, *Omar Takes on Responsibility and Accountability.*

- Discuss the informational interview. Have students present their career selections and why they are interested in their selections.

Homework due next week:

Assigned reading:

- Read Chapter 3, "Importance of Your Strengths."

Case homework:

- Read Case #8, *Teresa: Baking for Profit and Pleasure.* Answer all questions.

Week Four

Topics:

- Chapter 2, "How Systems and Organizations Work" (continued)

- Chapter 3, "Importance of Your Strengths"

- Chapter 4, "Making Transitions" (Intro)

Classwork:

- Discuss Case #8, *Teresa: Baking for Profit and Pleasure*, especially questions 4–6.

- Discuss "Importance of Your Strengths" (Chapter 3 Introduction).

- Read Case #9, *James Asks Lishone for a Raise.* Answer all questions, especially questions 4–9.

- Discuss sample budget.

- Read Exercise #3, *Presenting Your Strengths.*
- Read Chapter 4 in class and discuss transitions.
- Present overview of Case #10, *Fabiola: From Change to Transition.*
- Review the chart "Making Transitions."

Homework due next week:

Assigned reading:

- Re-read Chapter 4 and the chart "Making Transitions."

Case homework:

- Read Case #10, *Fabiola: From Change to Transition.* Assign questions.

Week Five

Topic: Chapter 4, "Making Transitions" (continued)

Classwork:

- Discuss Case #10, *Fabiola: From Change to Transition.*
- Discuss transition issues.

Homework due next week:

Assigned reading:

- Read Chapter 5, "Finding Mentors and Allies."
- Read Chapter 6, "Depersonalizing Issues and Recognizing the Needs of Others."

Case homework:

- Read Case #13, *Nat Wants to Change His Lunch Hour at Baldwin's Hardware* (revisited). Answer questions 4–9.
- Redo Exercise #3, *Presenting Your Strengths.* (By this time in the semester, students should be more confident and skilled at presenting their strengths. Because it is critical for self-advocacy and for their informational interview, we ask them to redo the assignment.)

Week Six

Topics:

- Chapter 5, "Finding Mentors and Allies"
- Chapter 6, "Depersonalizing Issues and Recognizing the Needs of Others"

Informational interview:

- Discuss how to get information about selected career field.

Classwork:

- Read Case #11, *David Moves Ahead.* Answer questions 3–7.

- Read Case #12, *Jasda Needs a Mentor.* Answer questions 1–6. Assign question 7 for extra credit.

- Read Case #13, *Nat Wants to Change his Lunch Hour at Baldwin's Hardware* (revisited). Answer questions 4–9; if time, answer 10–11.

- Read Case #14, *James Asks Lishone for a Raise* (revisited). Answer questions 4–6; if time, answer 7.

Homework due next week:

Assigned reading:

- Read Chapter 7, "Self-Advocacy Presentations."

Case homework:

- Read Case #15, *Ebony's Second Interview at E.L. Jenkins.* Answer questions 4, 5, 9, 11, 14.

Week Seven

Topic: Chapter 7, "Self-Advocacy Presentations"

Classwork:

- Review Chapter 7 Introduction.

- Discuss Case #15, *Ebony's Second Interview at E.L. Jenkins.* Answer questions 4–14, especially 6–8, 10, 12, 14.

- Read Case #16, *Cheyenne's Support.* Answer all questions.

- Read Case #17, *Tyshanna Needs Solutions.* Answer questions 4–8.

Homework due next week:

Assigned reading:

- Read Appendix A, "What Is an Informational Interview?"

- Read Appendix D, "Presentation Agendas."

Case homework:

- Read Case #18, *Trish Needs Informational Interviews in the Fashion World.* Answer all questions.

Informational interview homework:

- Have students develop a list of questions for their informational interviews.
- Continue collecting background information about career path.

Week Eight

Topic: Chapter 7, "Self-Advocacy Presentations" (continued)

Classwork:

- Answer questions about informational interview in Appendix A, "What Is an Informational Interview?"
- Discuss agendas in Appendix D, "Presentation Agendas."
- **Begin review of previous chapters.**
- Read Case #18, *Trish Needs Informational Interviews in the Fashion World.*
- Read Case #19, *Greta Writes a Letter.* Answer questions 4–7.
- Discuss questions for the informational interview.

Homework due next week:

Assigned reading:

- Read Appendix C, "Guidelines for Writing a Self-Advocacy Letter."

Case homework:

- Read Case #20, *Derek Gets an Informational Interview.*

Informational interview homework:

- Compose a letter to ask for an informational interview.
- Write the first draft of your informational interview agenda.

Week Nine

Topic: Chapter 7, "Self-Advocacy Presentations" (continued)

Classwork:

- Discuss Case #20, *Derek Gets an Informational Interview.* Answer questions 4–8 and analyze each exchange of dialogue.
- Review dynamics of informational interview.
- Discuss request letter for an informational interview.
- Discuss the informational interview agenda.
- Revisit transitional issues.

Homework due next week:

Assigned reading:

- Read Chapter 8, "Rules, Laws, and Rights."

Case homework:

- Read Case #21, *Country Depot Gives a Warning.* Answer questions 3–8.

Week Ten

Topics:

- Chapter 8, "Rules, Laws, and Rights"
- Chapter 7, "Self-Advocacy Presentations" (continued)

Classwork:

- Review informational interview agendas.
- Prepare for role-playing.
- Review Chapter 8 Introduction.
- Read Case #21, *Country Depot Gives a Warning.*
- Read Case #22, *Jill Battles Back.*

Homework due next week:

Assigned reading:

- Review your informational interview agenda.

Informational interview homework:

- Review Appendix D, "Presentation Agendas."
- Revise informational interview agenda.
- Prepare for role-playing.

Week Eleven

Topic: Self-Advocacy Presentations

Classwork:

- Role-play informational interviews.

Homework due next week:

Assigned reading:

- Review your informational interview agenda.

Informational interview homework:

- Go on the informational interview.

Week Twelve

Topic: Self-Advocacy Presentations

Classwork:

- Give feedback on the informational interview.

- Present final evaluation (45 minutes).

Introducing the Seminar to Your Students

Introductions

Ask students to introduce themselves by telling their name, what they like to do, and what career they think they would be interested in pursuing. Introduce yourself and tell the class how you came to be teaching this Seminar and why you like teaching it.

Introduction to the Seminar and Case Studies

You can use the Introduction of *On Your Own as a Young Adult: Self-Advocacy Case Studies* to introduce the class to the Seminar. This will give them an overview of the Seminar's content and style.

Who is the intended audience for this Seminar?

- For young adults who have goals for the future and want to take on responsibility

- For young adults who have faced significant challenges

Socratic Case Method

Explain the Socratic Case Method to the class.

Who is in charge of your learning here?

Are you willing to have your ideas and analysis challenged?

Are you willing to challenge my ideas?

Explain to students that they are going to read many cases about different aspects of self-advocacy, and they are going to answer questions and come to their own understanding of how to develop and use good self-advocacy skills.

Learning will come from engaging in the casebook and class discussion and using the Socratic Case Method.

Does that make you the student an active or passive learner?

Self-Advocacy

What is the meaning of self-advocacy?

Why does anyone need the support of others?

Why can't you just ask for support?

- Self-advocacy is a method for getting others to support you.

Does making a "convincing" presentation take skill? Discuss how you can tell when someone is making a convincing presentation.

- "Convincing" includes presenting personal strengths, appealing solutions, and incorporating the other party's goals.

- The components of self-advocacy are identifying facts, analyzing facts, understanding the other side's goals, and developing and making a convincing presentation.

Can you think of a time in the future when you will need self-advocacy?

- Self-advocacy is a process students will use their entire lives.

Do you think it is useful to learn about legal methods?

- The origin of self-advocacy is legal. Lawyers and negotiators use advocacy as part of their work.

Self-Advocacy Benefits

How important is it for you to take control of reaching your goals?

Do you think anyone else can get you to reach your goals?

Why is it better for you to be chiefly responsible for reaching your goals?

- Helps you take more control of your life and be an assertive rather than a passive player in planning your life

- Teaches how to take on more personal responsibility and fully utilize community support

- Focuses attention on individual strengths rather than problems

- Helps develop a more specific vision of your future

- Teaches how to set up, prepare for, and conduct an informational interview

- Creates familiarity with college-type education and prepares you to take college classes, if that is one of your goals

Self-Advocacy Process

Ask the class to look at the "Self-Advocacy Process" in the Introduction (page xi) and have students explain the meaning of each term in **bold**.

Why does the self-advocate need to research the goals of "the other side"?

Is "the other side" always in opposition to the self-advocate or hostile to the self-advocate? Explain.

Student Requirements

Student will have to learn through the Socratic Case Method. This method requires that students learn from analyzing cases and applying self-advocacy principles to these cases. This type of learning can be very challenging because the correct answer is not supplied. Instead, students will have to discover the answers for themselves.

What are the benefits of this type of education?

What are the challenges of this type of education?

Students will be required to read these cases, think about them, and answer questions. Explain to students that in the first year of law school, most law students find the case reading very difficult and feel they don't understand everything they are reading. Students may find they don't understand everything you read.

Why is it still important for you to engage in each assignment, despite any difficulty?

Briefing a Case

Everyone has the experience of hearing stories that are told well and stories that are told poorly. A good storyteller can convince the audience about the importance of the issues in the story. A good storyteller understands the story. He or she understands each character and the situations in which the characters are involved. It is important for negotiators, lawyers, and self-advocates to fully understand their stories and present arguments for their positions in a strong manner. Briefing a case is a useful method for making sure the self-advocate understands all the important facts and issues of "the story" and the challenges the characters face.

The cases (stories) contain two types of facts: *simple* and *complex*.

What is an example of a simple fact?

- What is the facilitator wearing?

What is an example of analysis of the simple facts to derive complex facts?

- Why is the facilitator wearing these clothes?

- What do you think the facilitator's goals are for this day?

- What strengths is the facilitator demonstrating through his or her choice of clothes?

- What don't we know about the facilitator that would help us understand how this class will be conducted?

- What do you think are the facilitator's goals for this class? How are they demonstrated?

- How have you (the student) demonstrated your goals so far in this class?

Informational Interview

Discuss with students these points about the informational interview:

- It is the final project of the semester because it will require use of self-advocacy skills and be of great help in developing plans for your long-term goals.

- You will meet with an expert in your chosen career field. The person will be able to answer your questions about the career field. The person may also be able to help you eventually get an internship or connect with other professionals in the field.

- These experts have not yet been selected. They will be recruited especially for each of you after you choose a career field during the third week.

- The experts will be asked to give just thirty minutes to help a young person get information about the career field. They will know nothing about you and their reason for doing the interview will most likely be because they enjoy their work and like talking about it.

- You each will meet with your expert by yourself at his or her workplace. At the informational interview, you will be completely on your own.

- This interview could be one of the most valuable experiences you have in preparing for your professional career goals.

- In addition to regular homework on the cases, you will be preparing for this interview throughout the semester.

CHAPTER 1

Planning for and Reaching Your Goals

Introduction

Ask students to recount some recent experience of planning:

- A day's schedule
- What to wear to work
- When to do homework

Why do you plan? What problems have you had when you didn't plan?

Do you find you plan more when you have goals that are important to you?

Is it easier to plan a party rather than your future? Why?

What is your favorite TV show? How much planning is necessary to write the script and do the taping? Why?

Getting information about a future career is very important. Discuss how it can be very hard and frustrating as well.

- Very often when we begin to get information about something as important as a career, we don't even know the right questions to ask or whom to turn to. This can be very frustrating.

Does anyone have examples of getting advice and information that confused them so much they wanted to give up? What is a solution for this problem?

- Do not be afraid.
- Ask people what questions you should be asking.
- Keep turning to experienced people to get more information.
- Remember, confusion is part of the process before you can make a decision.

Case #1

Importance of Establishing Goals

Choosing career or professional goals is not easy. Starting to think about career goals is one way to take the first steps to becoming an advocate for yourself. It is critical in setting goals that you have enough information about the benefits and challenges of the goals you select.

Background

Young people often assume their future life planning can be held off indefinitely. However, young people from challenging backgrounds rarely have the luxury to put off planning.

Your students will be in stronger positions to make the transition to successful independence if they can begin to develop goals and useful plans for achieving those goals **now,** before independence is forced upon them. This is a major goal of the semester.

Why is planning important? When important decisions are forced on to people with no time to properly plan, they often become trapped in difficult situations. Without proper planning, options become limited. Planning increases the likelihood of reaching long-term goals.

Young adults may not have enough knowledge or experience to properly commit to long-term career and personal goals. Nonetheless, a final career goal is not as important as **learning the process** for developing goals and making plans to reach these goals. By involving young adults in the planning process now, they learn the process and in some cases actually get a head start on planning for specific careers. Many of the goals students develop now will change. However, if they learn the **process** and gain experience in planning, they will be able to change goals much more effectively in the future.

Throughout this discussion, it is important to emphasize the idea that only by setting short-term goals can they make plans to achieve their long-term goals. Independence can be so demanding that without well-developed plans, they may become overwhelmed and limit their chances of achieving long-term goals.

Most critical to the goal establishing and planning process is getting useful information. In this case, it is useful to stress how much Shavone does not know and how much work she needs to do before she can make any decisions.

Case Discussion

Review Case #1 and the questions from the student casebook.

Below are some important questions to consider if not already discussed.

Does Shavone have enough information to make a decision about her long-term career goals?

- Some of Shavone's possible career choices require obtaining more information.

- The easiest career path (phone company) may seem the best choice, short-term, but may not meet Shavone's long-term goals. Therefore, even this path, which may be the easiest to achieve, requires Shavone to obtain new information.

Is it possible for Shavone to choose security as well as pursue her desire to do what she likes?

- For example, could Shavone get a job at the phone company and still pursue other interests and even go to college?

What issues do you have to weigh to make a decision about career goals?

- Work satisfaction.

- Income and lifestyle.

- Extent of education and experience needed for career.

- Short-term and long-term benefits.

- Recognizing your own strengths and weaknesses.

- What are your core values? How will this career goal support or detract from these values?

- Does this path offer new challenges as you develop experience?

- Is the goal exciting enough that you would make sacrifices to achieve it?

- The demands and benefits of different careers.

Will goals Shavone makes now be a waste of effort if, in the future, she changes her career goals? Explain.

- The work she does now will be valuable because she will have more experience setting goals.

- If she changes goals in the future, the work she has done now will help her learn the process of goal setting and enable her to do it more efficiently in the future.

- Usually, even new goals will have some elements of present goals.

What are different ways to find out about careers?

- Internet

  - Professional associations

  - Government/Labor Department

  - Specific companies in the field

- Professional journals

- Friends/family who may work or know someone who works in the field

- Informational interview with someone in the field

- School guidance counselor

- Colleges (specific departments or graduate schools)

Pre-Evaluation

Administer Pre-Evaluation Exam. The Pre-Evaluation can be found at www.jist.com/K1653/Appendices.pdf. Explain to the students the following:

- They have 30 minutes to complete the evaluation.

- They will probably not be able to complete all the questions.

- The purpose is to help you focus the semester's work.

- This pre-evaluative exam is a method to determine the progress for each student and class. A similar exam will be given at the end of the semester.

- The exam gives the students a preview of some of the material that will be covered during the semester.

Case #2

Importance of Planning to Reach Goals

Everyone has to prepare for many job interviews in their lives. When you are starting out, you have little experience with job interviews and you—like everyone else—will make mistakes. If you can learn from your mistakes and from others, you will get much better at job interviews. One goal is to learn how to prepare for a job interview and learn how to correct mistakes.

Background

Your students have a great deal of natural and developed talents. When they fail to reach a goal, it may be because they have failed to engage in significant planning. Most self-advocacy consists of a dialogue, or negotiation. Your students cannot be successful in this process unless they have adequate information that persuades the other party of the benefits of supporting a course of action. They must plan carefully for every self-advocacy presentation.

Ebony's first interview is typical of the way many students might approach this process. Interestingly, they will see some of Ebony's mistakes but may have trouble identifying lack of planning as a significant mistake. Most challenging to your students will be to devise a strategy for Ebony to gain Ms. Ward's support in the future.

The primary self-advocacy issues this case presents are the need to have

- Good information
- Well-thought-out goals
- Knowledge or analysis of the other party's needs and goals
- Ability to present one's strengths

Emphasize that these elements of effective self-advocacy need to be addressed to be successful.

What Is a Mutual Fund Company?

A *mutual fund* combines the money that many different individuals have saved and "invests" it in different corporations.

Investing consists of buying a small share of a corporation. If the corporation does well, this share can be sold for more money. If the corporation does poorly, the investor can lose all of his or her invested money. Investing has risks but it can help a person make more money from money he or she has saved.

- For example: Brian is a pastry chef. He wants to save money for his child's education and to continue his college education. He has saved $3,000 over 13 months of work and is thinking about moving it from his bank to a mutual fund. If the money is invested in good companies, Brian might expect to get almost 6% to 8% a year ($180–$240). There is a chance that Brian could lose his entire investment ($3,000) but the mutual fund has a good reputation for selecting solid companies. If Brian puts his money in a bank, he would get approximately 1.25% a year ($37.50). However, the bank deposit is totally safe. He can never lose his money.

Brian figures that investing will get him an extra $142.50 to $202.50 the first year and more than that the next year with "compounding." If he does not take out any money, and he averages 8% a year, in

- 5 years his $3,000 would be worth as much as $4,408
- 10 years it would be worth as much as $6,477
- 15 years Brian's original investment of $3,000 might be worth $9,517

If he left his $3,000 in the bank at 1.25% interest, he would only have in

- 5 years, $3,192
- 10 years, $3,397
- 15 years, $3,614

Because Brian doesn't need the money for the next five years, and the mutual fund will give a much larger return, he decides to take the risk and invest in the mutual fund.

Case Discussion

Review Case #2 and the questions from the student casebook.

Below are some important questions to consider if not already discussed.

What are the benefits of planning self-advocacy presentations to reach goals?

- Provides time for reflection and developing a strong presentation.
  - If Ebony had been more informed about E.L. Jenkins, she would have been able to communicate her strong desire to get an internship or job and connect this goal to advancing E.L. Jenkins's goals.

- Prepares you for the other party's questions.
  - Ms. Ward didn't really ask any questions that could not have been anticipated if Ebony had planned for the interview.

- Focuses on the most important self-advocacy elements.
  - Demonstrating her understanding of E.L. Jenkins's goals
  - Communicating her strengths and value for E.L. Jenkins
  - Presenting a solution that would benefit E.L. Jenkins and be easy to implement

- Keeps you focused on your objective during setbacks.

  - Ms. Ward was very focused on information she wanted and may have overpowered Ebony. If Ebony had a plan and an agenda, she might have been able to shift some of the conversation back to her agenda.

- Insures that you make your strongest points during your presentation.

  - Reduces nervousness during presentation

What false assumptions did Ebony make that resulted in such a bad interview?

- E.L. Jenkins may need workers, but that does not mean Ms. Ward will hire anyone willing to work. Even though Ebony may be qualified for the job, she must prepare to communicate reasons why she should be hired. She cannot assume Ms. Ward will discover them on her own.

  - Effective self-advocates try to analyze their own assumptions and recognize the other party may have different perspectives and needs.

An internship is usually an unpaid job experience. The experience is similar to an education or training where you learn about a job and the skills connected to the job. Often internships result in jobs; therefore, internships are worth planning for.

What is involved in planning to get an internship?

- Most importantly, you must get complete information about the employer.

What are the ways to get information about a prospective employer?

- Research in the library
- Internet, either directly about a specific company or general company type
- Friends (Brian) or family
- Information from the company

With a little research, you can find the company's **central mission and objectives** and the business's general nature. This will help you determine how you can support the employer's goals. Doing this research will distinguish you as someone highly motivated to support the company's needs.

Ebony has an impressive range of strengths, including overcoming many challenges.

If Ebony had planned for this interview, she would have been able to communicate her strengths.

Is it important to anticipate the questions you may be asked?

- If self-advocates prepare for questions, they will be better able to analyze the questions they are asked in an interview. Ebony should have been prepared for most of Ms. Ward's questions and done a better job of understanding what information Ms. Ward was trying to get.

Was Ebony knowledgeable about the mutual funds business?

Was Ebony knowledgeable enough to know how her strengths could support E.L. Jenkins's goals?

Is there anything Ebony could do now to be more successful getting an internship at E.L. Jenkins?

- **Situations are reversible.** Ebony could follow up with a letter and then call and supply specific answers to Ms. Ward's questions. She can overcome appearing unprepared by responding in a very prepared manner.

Is it important that Ebony was 22 minutes late because she was unfamiliar with the new neighborhood?

How does Ebony's lateness affect Ms. Ward?

What does Ebony's lateness say about her?

Is there anything Ebony could have done to prevent being late?

How would Ebony have reacted if she had arrived on time and Ms. Ward was late?

Why do you think Ms. Ward made the appointment at 8:30 a.m. rather than a more reasonable hour, such as 10:45 a.m. or 3:00 p.m.?

What are the responsibilities of a Human Resources Director?

What are a receptionist's responsibilities?

In studying the Ebony case, you can explore the issues of

- Having a future orientation
- Realizing challenging backgrounds come in many different patterns
- Networking with friends and businesses
- Getting somewhere on time
- Preparing for interviews
- Depersonalizing a situation

Further Discussion

If you have time, discuss mutual funds and finances:

Does this type of investing seem reasonable? What are the risks? What are the benefits and drawbacks?

Discuss the concepts of saving, interest, and investing.

Why is it important to save money?

- For contingencies and for larger goals. Savings can provide a certain degree of independence and freedom to pursue your goals.

Case #3

Making Specific Plans to Reach Goals

A strategy *is a more careful and specific plan of action. Making a strategy helps you anticipate the range of challenges and be better prepared to reach your goals through self-advocacy.*

Background

Planning for and achieving goals requires work. Success usually comes to those who plan a strategy. Important goals require that students have knowledge about their goals and about those who can help them achieve those goals. Students must analyze this information and then carefully plan to get others to support their goals. This plan becomes their strategy.

Young people often have little experience with deliberately planning a strategy, although they may instinctively make plans to achieve some of their goals. By helping students understand strategizing, you will help them become more effective in achieving complex goals.

Samantha might go to her supervisor and just say she no longer likes working in his department and wants a transfer. If she did, it would most likely communicate a rejection of her supervisor and lack of enthusiasm for her work. Further, it would provide no useful reason for C&E to change her work assignment.

On the other hand, if Samantha works on developing a strategy, she might recognize that she has something of value to offer C&E. A strategy would help her identify the most appropriate person to address when making her self-advocacy presentation. If effective in communicating how her strengths would help C&E, she might be more successful in achieving a promotion and switching assignments.

Case Discussion

Review Case #3 and the questions from the student casebook.

Below are some important questions to consider if not already discussed.

Role-Play

Divide the class into two or more groups. Ask each group to read and answer questions and then report to the class.

Next, assign Group A the task of developing reasons why C&E would not want to transfer Samantha to another position. Assign Group B the task of developing a self-advocacy approach for Samantha. After each group works out their plans, role-play the self-advocacy. Select "Samanthas" from Group A and select C&E representatives from Group B. (It is often useful to assign characters in role-play opposite from the person's character or, in this case, opposite what the students prepared. This will help them understand the other position.)

What are the biggest problems in figuring out a strategy for solving Samantha's problem?

- There is no "correct way" or specified approach to solve this problem.

- Achieving goals requires creative approaches with a lot of thinking and rethinking.

- Need more knowledge of C&E and Samantha's goals.

Many people in Samantha's situation might just give up.

Does Samantha have any grounds to support a promotion?

- Some investment in her has already been made. If she remains a productive employee, she will **benefit C&E** because she already has some knowledge of how C&E works. If C&E loses her, they will have to pay to train someone new and risk losing a new employee that may not stay or work out.

- C&E could possibly benefit from Samantha gaining business skills in college and, in the future, gain her services as a manager.

- Store morale may be diminished if good employees keep leaving.

- It would be good public relations to have satisfied employees with many friends and relatives who are potential customers.

You can develop a chart of Samantha's goals related to C&E goals. Here is a sample chart:

Samantha's Goals	C&E Goals
Wants to work with people	Requires good sales people and cashiers
College/steady job	Requires employee reliability and skill development
Business major	Need to provide a source for future employees
Psychology	Need to develop talented and knowledgeable management personnel
Ordering CDs for customers	Need to provide customers with a wide selection of CDs and electronic merchandise

What rules or laws, if any, apply to this situation?

- Not many laws apply to this situation.

- Perhaps an employee manual; therefore, need persuasive self-advocacy.

What would be the value of seeking a promotion even if Samantha is turned down? (What is the long-term value of self-advocacy?)

- Gets management to look at Samantha as someone with ambition and as someone who could be more useful to them.

- Demonstrates assertiveness and ability to work within the system.

- Communicates to her direct supervisor that Samantha has goals that need to be met to keep her at C&E.

- Self-advocacy is part of an extended process that often brings results over an extended period of time, not instantaneously.

What are the disadvantages ofseeking this promotion?

- Costly in Samantha's time and emotional energy.

- Could create bad feelings with her direct supervisor.

- She might be perceived as too aggressive and not a team player.

Do the possible benefits outweigh the possible disadvantages? Explain why.

- If you have a solid long-term plan, the decision whether to seek a change in job responsibility becomes easier to make.

Case #4

Using Fact Finding and Analysis to Set Goals

Decision-making—including establishing goals for your self-advocacy—requires good information and sharp analysis. The most effective self-advocates are highly skilled at seeking out good information and making insightful analysis (taking a number of complex facts and creating a simpler understanding) from that information.

Background

The most successful self-advocates are individuals who have the most information and know how to use it. Without sufficient information, a self-advocate cannot make realistic goals, plan for achieving those goals, or take actions to reach those goals.

It is often very challenging to convince students of the importance of information and therefore, research. "Gut" feelings and instinct often seem sufficient for making decisions and presentations to achieve a goal.

Part of the resistance to information gathering is that it appears hard, and students often do not know how to analyze the information once it is obtained. The legal profession is based on acquiring knowledge, making analyses, and then developing an advocacy approach. The costs for students are extremely high if they do not plan goals. Usually they will just drift into whatever comes their way if they do not plan. The statistics indicate this can have disastrous results in terms of losing independence and losing the chance to attain their potential.

In this case, there is plenty of information present, but there is also a significant amount missing. The skilled self-advocate will use the apparent information to identify missing information. If the self-advocate can be specific about the missing information, he or she will be more effective in planning to get this information.

Michael is faced with some expedient goals that may divert him from his long-term goals. If Michael decides to follow his uncle's advice, the path will be considerably harder than going to mechanic's training. In fact, it may seem overwhelming. This is a typical situation faced by students. The trick is to demonstrate that "overwhelming" does not equate with impossible and that long-term benefits may warrant the struggle.

Finally, there is the issue of **delayed gratification.** Most young adults have limited experience with the benefits of delaying their gratification and are intensely focused on immediate goals. It might be useful to lead a discussion on this topic. For example, discuss comparison shopping, getting an internship rather than hanging out, training for a better job, etc.

Have students identify an action they took where they got something better or more valuable because they waited.

This is also a good time to ask students to identify why they are taking this seminar. Point out how much they are deferring by taking this seminar.

Case Discussion

Review Case #4 and the questions from the student casebook.

Below are some important questions to consider if not already discussed.

Begin the discussion with delayed gratification.

What else could you do with the seminar and homework time and the time you use to think about the seminar?

Why are you using all this time you could use for other things you want to do? Can you identify some specific benefits?

Now that they have identified the benefits, add the issue of risk—the heart of delayed gratification.

What are the risks of devoting all this time?

Could the seminar not work?

Could the informational interviewer not be helpful?

Perhaps there is a **little** risk. Point out that the students are making risks/benefits assessment when they delay gratification.

Model Fact Finding

The following is the "ideal" we look for in the student's ability to identify all the facts relevant to the issue. At this point in the semester, you might take the approach of breaking down this case in class as follows.

What specific facts do you presently know?

Michael's issue:

- Should he begin a training program to become a mechanic or go to college?

Michael's strengths:

- Wanted to work in the car business since he was five years old
- Specifically wants to own a car dealership
- Has done well in a high school science class
- Liked by his teachers
- Liked by friends
- Has a positive nature
- Responsible to his daughter and her mother

Michael's weaknesses:

- In some areas, such as schoolwork, needs to work harder

Michael's family:

- Sue
  - Daughter's mother
  - Plans to marry in one year

- Daughter
  - Six months old
  - Plans to maintain close family relationship with her

- Uncle Jordan
  - Lives in San Diego
  - Automobile brake specialist at a large car dealership
  - Liked by Michael a great deal
  - Visited by Michael every six months
  - Seems to be a source for useful advice in Michael's selected career field

What are the merits of taking a car repair training program?

- Would be earning a salary after only two months
- Would begin to get experience as a mechanic

What are the negatives of taking a car repair training program?

- Might miss out on going to college
- May limit long-term opportunities
- Have to move to another area of the country (giving up friends and family)

What are the merits of going to college?

- Increase long-term opportunities.
- Increase likelihood of reaching goal of owning or managing a car dealership.
- Increase earning opportunities.
- Recommended by uncle (opinion leader) who Michael respects.
- Michael is very well-liked and will probably be able to go far with a college education.
- More opportunity to change professional fields.

What are the negatives of going to college?

- Has had problems with schoolwork
- May limit short-term earning potential
- Additional expenses
- Puts off starting work in chosen profession

What other information do we need or what questions should we ask?

- Is the training a quality program?

- What education, experience, and position must one have to manage or own a car dealership?

- If Michael has done poorly in high school, can he do well in college?

- How can Michael support himself and his daughter while in college?

Which facts are most important for Michael?

We should analyze each fact as we identify them. What kind of categories would be good for distinguishing the value and nature of each fact? Does the fact go toward

- Strengthening the reason to pursue one of the career paths?

- Weakening the reason to pursue one of the career paths?

- Supporting Michael's ability to support the goals of owning a car dealership?

Do some decisions about short-term goals affect your success in achieving long-term goals?

- How do you identify such decisions?

- How do you calculate the pros and cons?

- Are there ways to combine immediate pragmatic decisions with strategies for achieving long-term goals?

Is Michael fortunate to have an uncle who helps him learn more about a career in the automobile field?

What are some ways for you to find such people in your life? (Bring in the use of informational interviews. Meeting such individuals can be invaluable as resources for information even if they cannot directly get one a job.)

- Taking advice is always an art form. It requires being open to new and different points of view and respecting the wisdom that comes from experience and age. At the same time, specific advice may not always be completely applicable to your situation. The advice taker must weigh advice and determine how to plan his or her goals and strategies. The ability to discriminate amongst differing advice comes with doing a lot of research and getting information from a wide variety of resources.

Exercise #1

Identifying Your Long- and Short-Term Goals

In order to get important information and begin planning for your future, it is useful to begin thinking of career and personal goals now. Write out your answers to the following questions. You may not know the answers to all the questions but do the best you can.

Background

To help students prepare for their futures, you need to help them build a vision of their futures. To build an obtainable vision, students need to learn to be more specific about their futures. This is a challenge. It requires careful introspection as well as knowledge about future goals and possible paths to reach those goals.

The exercise's purpose is to introduce students to the process of thinking about their futures. Students need to understand that they must go beyond simply identifying a career or future goal, and they need to be specific about their goals. Students also need to understand that achieving long-term goals requires establishing short-term goals.

Questions

1. **Long-Term Goals**

   a. What type of job or career will you be working toward in five years?

   b. Where will you be living in five years?

   c. What will be the most important changes you will have to make in your life to reach these goals?

2. **Short-Term Goals**

   a. What things will you have to do to reach your career goals?

   b. What are your education goals?

   General   High School

                     College

                     Specific training (technical or trade school)

   Specific   What major will you select in college?

                     What other training will you need?

                     What books should you read?

                     What specific skills do you need to learn?

                     What other sources of career information do you need to look at?

                     Who would you want to have informational interviews with?

Many individuals take jobs that are not specific 5-year career goals, but are important steps to reaching their goals. For example, you many have to take a job to support yourself while you work toward your long-term career goals. Or you may take a job or internship to gain experience and contacts for your long-term job goals.

Think about this and try to identify short-term job and internship goals you might have before you reach your long-term career goal.

Example: "My long-term career goal is to sell advertising for a music magazine. I need to get a college education to learn about business and to improve my ability to understand and communicate with others. While I'm going to college, I want to work at a magazine, newspaper, or media company in their sales or advertising department to learn more about the business and earn enough money to support myself through college. While in college, I'll take any job, such as a receptionist, messenger, or clerk, at a magazine, newspaper, or media company just to be around people who work in the field and make contacts even if that job is not exactly what I want."

Discussion

This exercise has critical importance. It begins to focus the student on his or her long-term career goal. The outcome will determine the expert selected for the student's informational interview. Therefore, help the students to carefully engage with this exercise.

Try to get students to be as specific as possible in answering the questions.

For some questions, students will not be able to provide any specifics. Use these instances to demonstrate why getting the missing information will be important to them.

After some discussion, ask students to complete the exercise in writing. Then ask them to take it home, carefully consider their responses, and rewrite any answers for submission for next week.

Why is it important now to know what specific skills you will need to reach your future goals?

- You can begin working on developing some of these skills now.

- You can begin to plan how you can learn these skills and find appropriate schools, training programs, internships, etc.

If you have a choice between making more money with one job and gaining more experience for your future career with another job that pays less, how would you make the decision?

- Money is a real concern and unless you know how much you will need, you can't make this decision.

- Experience for a career is extremely important and will provide long-term benefits and security that will make up for the discrepancies in pay now. If you took the lower-paying job but it gave you experience that would help you get a better job that paid $7,500 more a year five years from now, then the decision is an easy one.

- You can't make the decision to take the lower-paying job that provides you with experience unless you are willing to cut your expenses and make some sacrifices, such as having a roommate, going out less, putting off buying some clothes, taking a second job, etc.

Why should you be thinking about your future educational goals now?

- If you know now what education you will need, you can begin to look for scholarship and financing opportunities, learn and prepare for admissions requirements, talk with teachers about the best preparation, and begin to make budgeting plans for your future.

Why should you be thinking now about future goals that are five or more years ahead of you?

- There is a great deal of preparation that you can do now in order make sure you reach your goals. Planning your housing, finances, education, training, and jobs are all major efforts that can make the difference between reaching or failing to reach your long-term objectives.

- Even if you change your mind, you will have begun to learn the process of preparing for long-term goals, and it will be easier to work on any new plans.

At this point, students may not be able to answer all the questions in the exercise. However, exposure to the questions will prompt them to start thinking about a broader range of issues and prepare them to focus on important issues for their informational interview.

Informational Interview

Ask students to think about some decision they have made in their lives that was influenced by information they received from someone else; for example, making a purchase, selecting a meal, choosing a high school elective or teacher, seeing a movie, selecting a CD, etc.

Why did you seek or take someone else's advice?

Why did you respect this person's information and advice?

Did you take all the advice and give up any thinking on your part?

Would you ask that person again for additional information?

- Getting information and advice from knowledgeable and experienced people is one important way we learn.

What is the purpose of an informational interview?

- Get information

- Learn about a career

- Learn how to prepare to train for that career

- Have an opportunity to self-advocate for yourself and gauge feedback

- Make a potential contact for future help in getting an internship, job, or connecting to others in the career field

Why is it important to select a specific career field now?

- This is a fantastic opportunity to talk with a very experienced professional. The time you spend to prepare for this interview will be considerable. Therefore, you don't want to waste your effort.

- Carefully think about a specific career field you have a passion for. Even if you are not certain, make a decision so you can benefit from this opportunity.

- Do not be embarrassed about your selection. There is no best career. The challenge is to find a career field from which you will get satisfaction.

- Changing your mind is permissible!!! At this interview, you may get information that will help change your mind. This is great because it is helping you to narrow your focus and to learn more about what you want to do so you can start preparing now.

Tell a colleague's story or your own experiences selecting a career field. Demonstrate the importance of getting information from knowledgeable and experienced people in the career field.

CHAPTER 2

How Systems and Organizations Work

Introduction

Start with a discussion of what organizations your students are a part of.

What organizations are you part of?

- High school

- After-school sport or program

- Family or group home

Break the class into a few groups representing different organizations they have identified. Ask each group to work on the following questions and make a report to the class.

Have students identify how the organization works.

What are the organization's goals?

How do individuals in the organization benefit from the organization?

Do individuals in the organization ever make decisions based on what is best for the organization? If so, how does that benefit them?

Are different people in the organization responsible for specific areas?

Have students discuss the Chantel example from the reading at the beginning of the chapter.

- Does Chantel have reasonable personal work goals? Explain.

- Has Chantel done a good job connecting her personal work goals with the organization's goals? Explain.

- Discuss goals and needs of the other side.

- Discuss why a good attorney or advocate must understand the other side's position in order to make a strong advocacy case. By understanding the other side's position, the attorney or advocate

  - Anticipates the most convincing arguments

  - Understands areas for possible agreement

- Anticipates areas of greatest resistance

- Helps make his or her own goals more specific

- Most people and organizations are interested in their own goals and not yours.

- Most people in charge must focus on their organization's goals before paying attention to your goals.

- People in a position to help you have a large range of goals and needs. It is your job to try to identify these goals and needs.

- Some goals and needs can be deduced and others can be researched, if not from a specific person, then from the organization or profession he or she represents.

Discuss Homework

Make some general remarks about areas that demonstrate good engagement in the work and areas that need more work. Stress that you are not looking for correct answers as much as

- Thoughtful consideration of the question

- Specific responses rather than generalities

- Analysis of the issues and information supported by **specific** facts from the case and knowledge gained from the seminar

Use some student homework to demonstrate good answers. Even an academically weak student may have a portion of an answer that demonstrates intellectual engagement. Using such an example publicly will encourage the student. Without singling out specific students, seriously discuss the consequences of not doing homework or falling behind:

- Learning comes from engaging in the cases through homework as well as classwork.

- To be well-prepared for and benefit from an informational interview, you must be a skilled self-advocate. Homework is essential for this preparation.

- Real understanding comes from empowerment and taking responsibility for using your own intellect. Doing homework facilitates this objective. If you have a problem with homework for any reason, you must see the facilitator.

- Invite students to suggest additional approaches they believe would help them improve their understanding of the self-advocacy process. This is a good time to explain the value of the Socratic Method. Explain that it is not useful to get answers from you, nor are you always correct. Rather, students must engage in the material and discussion and come to their own reasoned conclusions that make sense to them.

Exercise #2

Organizations' Missions

All organizations have missions. *A mission can be thought of as an organization's overall or long-term goal. Whether you want to get a job, join a group, or work with an organization, you need to understand the organization's mission.*

Background

For some students, understanding how organizations work may be the hardest learning objective of the semester. Students typically have little experience with organizations other than public schools, foster care agencies, or other government systems. These systems are unlike most organizations they will encounter in the future.

This exercise helps students learn that all organizations have a specific purpose or mission and that all decisions made by people acting on behalf of the organization relate to this mission. If students can fully understand the organization's mission, then it becomes easier for them to make self-advocacy presentations with solutions that benefit the organization.

It is natural for students to have difficulty connecting the organization's overall business profit needs with the organization's unique marketing approach. For example, in *Jamal Finds the Missions*, R.B. Plumbing has an overall need to make a profit. While there is not much information in the case, students should be encouraged to deduce that the specific marketing approach is to gain customers by demonstrating competitive and reasonable prices, thus the offer of free estimates. It is important to note that the mission must go beyond just making money and include some specific approach that distinguishes an organization from a competing organization.

Students will often probe further and suggest that R.B. Plumbing has a need to provide quality plumbing to make customers feel at ease with their plumbing systems, or make customers feel that R.B. is always available to fix any plumbing problem. But in returning to the stated facts, pricing appears to be the major marketing objective.

Jamal Finds the Missions

When Jamal was 19, he was all on his own, except for a friend who got him a night job at a large package delivery company in Houston, Texas. He quickly realized the work was hard and boring and not something he would want to do the rest of his life. He decided he would have to go to college in order to get a better education and the opportunity to get a more interesting job.

Going to college was very difficult for Jamal. He had to get financial aid, borrow money, and work part-time. The college work was much more difficult than high school. While he was in college, a number of his teachers commented on his ability to make people feel comfortable. A marketing teacher suggested he go into sales because he was good with people and was also very good at understanding other people's needs.

(continued)

(continued)

Jamal now works as a salesperson for Program Designs (PD), a computer programming company. (Computer programs are ways workers can use their computers to do important things for their business. For example, a computer program can plan the best route for a delivery truck making many deliveries.) PD designs custom software (computer programs) to help businesses save time and work more efficiently. Jamal's job is to sell PD's services to different organizations.

Jamal is lining up a number of businesses that might benefit from PD's custom software. His plan is to have two meetings with these potential clients (business customers). Jamal will call each business and ask whether he can meet with their top executives. At this first meeting, Jamal will find out about the **needs** of the business, what products they sell, how they sell these products, what they identify as their long-term goals, and whether they have any problems with running the business.

Within two weeks after this first meeting, Jamal will follow up with a presentation of a plan for custom software that will help the company save time and money and increase efficiency in order to reach their long-term organizational goals. He will also explain PD's services and costs.

Jamal knows that getting the first meeting to collect specific information is the hardest step. To get this meeting, he will have to demonstrate at least some overall understanding of the organization's needs and mission.

Example

Jamal thinks that R.B. Plumbing would benefit from PD's services. He knows that R.B. Plumbing offers free estimates (informing how much it will cost the customer) to customers considering plumbing jobs. This is a big advantage to customers because other plumbers charge by the hour plus materials and don't give any estimate of how much the job will cost. Thus, a customer might pay much more than he or she expected when the job is completed.

If PD can develop software that will reduce the time it takes to make estimates and make the estimates more accurate, it will save R.B. Plumbing time and money. Because Jamal knows that the main way R.B. gets customers is through free estimates, Jamal will call R.B. Plumbing and ask them if they would be interested in a service that would help them save time and be more accurate in making estimates. Jamal is confident that they will want the software he is selling. Jamal believes R.B. Plumbing will be interested in a meeting where Jamal can learn about R.B. Plumbing's specific needs and then present his solutions.

Question

The following is a list of the organizations Jamal intends to contact. For each one, he needs to understand the mission of the organization so he can offer valuable computer software. Try to analyze what you think the mission is for each of the following companies. All these organizations want to make a profit (money), but ask yourself, "How does each organization want to accomplish this goal? How does each one make their organization stand out and be different from the rest?"

- The PAG, a specialty clothing and accessory chain of stores
- Phil's Bakery, specializing in eight different types of bread and specialty muffins

- C&E Electronics, selling popular electronics and small appliances
- ENVY, a dance club
- Hannibal Bookstore, specializing in self-help books

Discussion

It is essential that students understand organizations have goals just as individuals do. Understanding those goals can be instrumental in helping a student become a successful self-advocate. Thus, this simple exercise has critical importance.

Break the class into two or more groups. Assign each group two or more example organizations and have them work on the specific goals (mission) for each organization. Have them report to the class and push them to be specific in defining missions.

How does the organization's mission distinguish itself from other organizations doing similar things?

For example, what would be the distinction between Virgin and Circuit City's mission in selling CDs?

- Both make a profit selling music CDs
- Perhaps one store focuses on a different music type
- Perhaps one store provides more customer service and knowledge about music
- Perhaps one store greatly outdoes the other in price

As we learn these distinctions, we can better understand how to approach Tower Records with the self-advocacy presentation.

Share the mission of Tower Records.

If you look online at the Tower Records Web site, you will find information that can help you figure out its mission. Tower Records views itself as the most diverse source for selling entertainment including CDs, videos, books, and even eclectic art. The store prides itself on its diversity of entertainment media, which is reflected in its employee diversity. It believes diversity helps it remain at the cutting edge of the industry. Service and selection is a primary objective.

Knowing this would help an employee who wants a promotion to "product buyer." A product buyer determines what products local customers desire and then places the orders and follows through to see that the products arrive in the store.

In any self-advocacy presentation to get a promotion, the self-advocating employee might emphasize the diversity in his or her background, friends, and interests (wide range of understanding books, music, videos, and art) as well as an ability to remain current with the popular scene and use organizational skills related to the ordering process.

Case #5

Matching Your Goals with the Needs of an Organization

Often when you need something from an organization, you have to negotiate with a supervisor. This can be frustrating when that person seems to have a lot on his or her mind and doesn't really care about what you want or need. Trying to understand what that person is concerned about can help you reach your goals.

Background

Many young adults might empathize with Nat if they didn't know the other facts related to the characters in the scene. Nat has two fundamental problems. He does not recognize the needs and goals of the others in the case, and he does not understand the structure of the hardware store.

Nat assumes Alicia has unlimited power. He also doesn't understand that she is accountable for employee coverage and a range of other things that weigh heavily on her mind. Even if Nat had presented his request at a better time, he still needs to understand Alicia's role in the entire store and find ways to support Alicia's job goals. Better understanding the store's structure would help.

Often it seems no one cares about someone else's situation. Successful self-advocacy and goal attainment requires individuals to diminish their emotions about the people involved. The self-advocacy process helps one **depersonalize** the issues at stake and make a much stronger presentation. This exercise helps to demonstrate that a supervisor's negative reaction to a request is often related to his or her own business and personal needs rather than liking or disliking the requestor.

Of critical importance for Nat is his ability to recognize he has talents and services of value to Baldwin Hardware. His future goal of working in construction may likely demonstrate that he has skill and aptitude for mechanical things related to hardware. Nat might be a real asset for helping customers solve hardware-related problems and helping out at the Thursday tool instruction.

This is also a good case to practice fact-finding. There are some details embedded in the story that will make for some creative solutions for Nat. The self-advocate will have to work hard to find them.

Case Discussion

Review Case #5 and the questions in the student casebook.

Following are some important questions to consider if not already discussed.

Can you analyze the story's facts to understand two important elements, the store's structure and the character's needs?

It would be useful to understand all the characters in the situation to make a sound analysis. Look at each character's work-related and, to a lesser extent, personal needs. This is a good practice for analyzing any situation when preparing to self-advocate.

Alicia's Role and Individual Goals

Role

- Runs an efficient work schedule for Baldwin Hardware to properly serve its customers and make a profit
- Has supervisory responsibilities and needs to demonstrate she can do all her assigned work well
- Has range of responsibilities, from running the cash register to interacting with customers
- Manages activities when Danielle, the manager, is off the customer floor
- Is trusted to run cash register without direct supervision of the manager

Individual Goals

- Go to college
- Make more money
- Leave home
- Impress Danielle with her professionalism
- Motivate customers to return to the store
- Reduce her anxiety level by limiting any extra work or changes she has to make

Other Considerations

- Harassed by her mother and Danielle
- Under pressure from customers, particularly Tanya
- Probably depressed by boyfriend's death
- Under pressure to keep accounts accurate as she works the cash register
- Under pressure to schedule employees; this is a relatively new assignment and she is overly anxious about it
- Does not make enough money to support her goals
- Feels anxious about asking Danielle for help
- May not react well to hot days

Nat's Role and Individual Goals

Role

- Stock clerk in small hardware store

- Identifies many hundreds of items

- Restocks items as they are returned

- Helps find merchandise for customers

- Is very helpful if he knows how items are used

- At busy purchasing times, such as lunch hours, may have to work extra hard in restocking purchased items and finding items for customers

- Has potential to contribute to the Thursday night demonstrations because of his own familiarity with construction and hardware

Individual Goals

- Open own construction company

- Gain experience and funding to begin company

- May need some flexible scheduling to begin some private construction work

- Shift lunch schedule

Other Considerations

- Preoccupied with helping friend

- Focused on long-term career goal with a specific plan to achieve it

Danielle's Role and Individual Goals

Role

- Manages the store

- Responsible for all activities of store, including

  - Maintaining a large range of items customers might need

  - Making Baldwin Hardware an attractive store for customers

  - Managing budget and payroll, as well as paying suppliers, landlord, and taxes

  - Making and keeping track of profit, especially as she is probably paid according to profit

  - Advertising

  - Making Baldwin Hardware responsive to customers' needs

  - Hiring, training, and keeping good employees (or dismissing bad ones)

Individual Goals

- Run a good hardware store and make a profit

- Delegate responsibility

Other Considerations

- Stressed from responsibilities of running store and perhaps other aspects of her life we don't know about

Why might Nat consider getting involved in the Thursday evening tool instruction?

- Increase his chance to successfully start a construction company
- Learn more about tools
- Learn more about the customers' needs
- Meet professionals who run the instruction
- Demonstrate commitment to job
- Position himself for a more flexible time schedule
- Demonstrate a willingness to learn more about the hardware business
- Become more valuable for Baldwin Hardware

Case #6

Organizational Structure

At every organization there is a chain of command. *When you advocate for yourself, it's critical to know who is in charge of specific functions of the organization. Otherwise, you might spend your time trying to persuade the wrong person to help you.*

Background

Young adults often have the experience of not getting a satisfactory response or assistance from a professional. This causes a great deal of frustration. Often young adults think hiring an attorney would be the only way to protect their rights or receive any assistance. Rarely does a young adult identify the power he or she does have, which often comes from helping the other person reach some of his or her goals or needs.

Here, Smoothée may have little power, he may be incompetent, or he may even have some ax to grind. We are advised that coercion through legal means will probably not work even though there is a legal contract. Latoya must analyze the organization's structure and the power she has within this structure. Then if she can identify the right person in the organization who will understand how Hipazz can benefit Renraw, Hipazz may finally resolve its problem.

Case Discussion

Review Case #6 and the questions in the student casebook.

Below are some important questions to consider if not already discussed.

This is a good case for experiencing the analysis process of preparing for self-advocacy.

Step #1: What reasons would Renraw have to support Hipazz? To which of the company's goals do they relate?

What are Renraw's goals?

1. Signing new groups and keeping groups signed that have the potential to produce hits. This might be apparent if there is

   - A division at the recording company responsible for finding, recruiting, and signing new groups

   - Someone of importance who is in charge of this division—usually a Vice President in charge of...

   - A department called "talent department," "artist development," etc.

2. Getting more sales from albums.

   - Most recording companies have "sales departments." Who is in charge of this sales department? Usually a Vice President in charge of...

3. Increasing good public relations.

   - Benefit from future publicity in magazines.

   - Hipazz already has a track record.

4. Creating a good public image for other successful music groups.

Step #2: Find out who is in charge of each identified division (for example, new artists, sales, promotion, engineering, production, etc.).

One of the first steps in the self-advocacy process is to identify who is the best person to hear your presentation. This step must come before actually making your full self-advocacy presentation.

Selecting the right person to present your case to can often be the most important element contributing to your success. Selecting the wrong person can, at best, lead to no help for your position and, at worst, lead to active resistance, which will lengthen the time it takes to reach your goal.

If someone has accountability, he or she is responsible for the success of an organization's division and needs to act in a manner that brings success. This means that if you can demonstrate how doing something will help support this person's responsibilities, there is a good chance he or she will support your presentation.

Step #3: Try to find out something about these people.

- Talk with other recording artists.

- Talk with friends working at Renraw.

- Talk with friends in the industry.

- Look at past records of individuals. What else has Renraw produced? Was it successful? How long has the sales manager been with the company? What is her record?

- Go to others in the company seeking advice rather than complaining.

Step # 4: Just in case nothing else works, find out who is in charge of running the entire company.

Ask students to describe the organization of a music company. As they develop the elements of the organization, draw an organizational chart on the board using the guide below.

Example: Renraw Music, Inc.

The following might resemble the structure of a well-sized music recording company:

- **Marketing and Sales**

  Design the strategy and execute it to get the most CDs sold to CD retailers, broadcasters, and others who play CDs and videos.

- **Advertising**

  Place advertisements in appropriate media for targeted audiences.

- **Public Relations**

  Create and promote good stories about artists and companies.

- **Art Department**

  Create covers and any of the graphics, photos, etc., used for advertising, public relations, and CD packing. Also help develop videos.

- **Promotion**

  Develop ways of promoting artists and Renraw's music through concerts, booking appearances by artists, etc.

- **Artist Development**

  Implement Renraw's strategy for defining specific musical sounds, finding artists that fit into this category, and selecting those who will be successful.

- **Artist Management**

  Assign associate producers such as Smoothée to be responsible for supporting the artists, arranging their work, and ensuring that their recordings reach everyone's goals.

- **Production**

  Arrange all recordings and ensure top quality. May also arrange for the actual production (duplication) of the CDs.

- **Financial**

  Control the budget and make financial projections. Also monitor all the expenditures and income of the company.

- **Facility**

  Take care of the buildings, phones, mail delivery, support staff, security, janitorial work, etc.

- **Human Resources**

  Find and hire employees and support their needs.

- **Administrative**

  Coordinate all departments to make sure the central mission is supported throughout the company. Make all the major decisions.

What is a chain of command?

Remember that most organizations have a structure. People are responsible for specific things. Also, most people have supervisors, and those supervisors have supervisors, all the way up to the head of an organization, creating the *chain of command*. Other terms are *hierarchy, power structure,* and *pecking order.*

When you have a problem with an organization (foster care agencies, school, etc.), to whom do you go? How do you decide?

In planning to whom to go,

1. Make a list.

   - Who (name and title) is responsible for the specific problem you are having?

   - Is there a person with authority and accountability that would understand how helping you would benefit his or her organization?

   - Who are the people (and their positions/titles) who appear most responsive to you or others with similar problems?

   - Who in the organization has little power?

   - Who in the organization is the most negative? (Is this true or just reputation? If reputation, how reliable is it?)

2. Develop a plan of what order you should see people to seek a resolution for your problem.

   - You should be prepared to go to more than one person to get full support for your proposal.

   - You may have to develop allies within the organization who can support your ideas with the decision-maker.

Case #7

Accountability

Accountability *usually means that a person is identified as responsible for some activ-ity or the results of some activity within an organization.*

It doesn't make sense to go to a store and try to return a pair of shoes to the security guard. Therefore, when you advocate for yourself, it is important to understand who on the other side is accountable.

Organizations have many activities and responsibilities. Because these activities are important and because they require other people, machines, and services, one person will be made in charge to manage these activities. That person makes decisions, spends money, makes sure everything goes the way it should, and that everyone involved is doing the right thing. That person is considered "accountable" for the success of that activity, **even if they do not personally do all the activities themselves.**

Taking on accountability often results in special recognition and promotions within the organization. At the same time, if things do not work out, the person in charge will be held "accountable" for problems and failures. This can result in being denied promotions, not receiving a raise in salary, or even being dismissed from a job.

Background

Accountability may not be well-understood by some students. The idea of having responsibility for other people's actions and events, over which one does not always have direct control, can seem unreasonable or unfair. While accountability creates risks, it also allows one to take some control of his or her job and gain benefits.

Understanding accountability can be useful for the self-advocate. It helps them direct their presentations at the appropriate person and not waste time going to an individual who cannot be of any help.

Examples of Accountability:

If a school continues to have students perform poorly on academic tests, the principal, Mr. Graham, may be replaced with another person. Even though the principal doesn't teach the classes and isn't directly responsible for the behavior of the students, he will be held accountable for the poor results. In such a situation, the principal may be asked to provide a reason why the results are so poor and a good plan for improving conditions. Mr. Graham may even be given a time limit as to when the results must improve or else he will be replaced.

Accountability occurs even in family life. If Karaar has an eight-year-old child, he is accountable for the health and education of his child. Karaar might want to quit his job until he finds one he really loves, but the loss of income may prevent his child from eating well, having the necessary clothes, or doing well in school. Karaar might want to come home late every night and not help his child with his schoolwork, yet the teacher has told him that his child needs Karaar's help with homework each night. In this case, the accountability is more self-imposed, but nevertheless, Karaar is accountable for his child.

Accountability gets very complicated sometimes. If Karaar's child is in Mr. Graham's school, and Karaar is not helping his child with homework even though the teacher recommended it, is Mr. Graham or Karaar responsible for the child's poor achievement?

Case Discussion

Review Case #7 and the questions in the student casebook.

Below are some important questions to consider if not already discussed.

Describe what it means to be accountable in an organization.

- Someone who is accountable for a large range of responsibilities typically has the power to make important decisions for an organization.

- Accountability implies one can be penalized as well as rewarded for the results of his or her work. Those with accountability need great assurance that their decisions will result in achieving desired goals.

- If someone is accountable, they will be held responsible for the successes and failures of people who work for them.

- Accountable people are always looking for ways to achieve success in their areas of responsibility. Anyone who has a good solution for contributing to success will usually be listened to and often supported.

Most of your self-advocacy will be conducted with people who have accountability.

What are some indicators of accountability within an organization?

- **Money/Budgets**

    Usually accountability requires control of budgets (the authorization to spend the organization's money for particular goods and services) and the ability to decide how to spend money.

- **Knowledge**

    Usually individuals who are made accountable have a good deal of knowledge and experience in their job areas.

- **Titles or positions of authority**

    Individuals with accountability are usually identified within an organization with executive (top) job titles, such as CEO, President, Vice President, Manager, Supervisor, Account Executive, etc.

You can often find out who is responsible (accountable) for specific activities or decisions by calling the main office and just asking. People who are accountable in an organization are usually the same people who can be helpful in supporting your objectives. They are usually **"decision-makers"** as well as **"opinion leaders."**

In the case, Omar has become store manager. Many employees in the store have responsibilities similar to the ones Omar had when he was working his way up to manager. Now that Omar is manager, he not only has responsibilities, but he is accountable.

For example:

- If the produce manager purchases rotten fruit and the store loses $5,000 in sales because they cannot sell produce one day, Omar will be held accountable by the company he works for. They will assume he poorly managed the produce section. Conversely, if the store gets a great reputation for the produce selection made by the produce manager and sales increase $1,000 a day, Omar will get credit for this success.

- Jill's broken arm is the direct fault of the shift maintenance person. But if Jill sues the store, Omar will be held accountable. If no one has accidents in the store, Omar will be recognized as a capable store manager.

- If people get sick from prepared food sold by the store, Omar will be held accountable. Whether the food is prepared by the deli staff or purchased from an outside service, Omar will be held accountable for the store's loss in reputation, possible law suits filed by people who became sick, and loss in revenue (sales). Conversely, if the prepared food is always fresh and desirable and more customers are attracted to the store by the quality of the prepared food, sales will increase and Omar will be given credit.

- It is more confusing as to who is accountable for someone getting food poisoning from canned food. Clearly, the food is prepared and canned by a manufacturer that is not under the control of Omar or his store. If the canned food is from a company with a high reputation, most likely Omar will not be held accountable. Yet, if the food company is not well-known, the fact that Omar's store decided to sell this brand will be viewed negatively and Omar will be held accountable.

Anything that affects the reputation and sales in Omar's store is ultimately his responsibility, and thus, he is the person who is held accountable.

Does this appear fair? Why?

Is there anything for which you didn't directly have responsibility for but were held accountable anyway?

Why was it both fair and unfair to have held you accountable?

Informational Interview Discussion

Ask each student to read his or her long-term career goal and explain what he or she finds attractive about it.

Lead a discussion on the best ways to get background information about these careers. Explain how this information will help them ask better questions at their interviews, get more specific information, and demonstrate their motivation.

Think of sources.

- Guidance counselors
- Professional associations
- Government Labor Department
- Colleges
- Professional journals
- Informational interviews

Outline the basic information one could get from some of these sources.

- Nature of the job
- Required training, education, and experience
- Outlook for career field in future
- Geographic areas of concentration
- Possibilities for advancements
- Salary range

Case #8

Analyzing the Needs of an Organization

Sometimes it seems that your boss will never understand that you deserve more—a salary increase, a vacation, a change in schedule, etc. Analyzing the goals of the organization you work for and demonstrating how your goals will support the organization's goals will help you be a successful self-advocate.

Background

Young adults in the public school system, after-school programs, and the foster care system experience organizations with a central value of looking after childrens' needs. Many youth in these systems naturally see the world as responsible for responding to their needs. Because of this experience, many youth are unprepared to accept or understand that individuals outside the education and child welfare systems respond to their personal goals and to the goals of the organizations they represent.

This concept often draws resistance from students. "It doesn't seem fair." Perhaps it isn't fair, but it is a reality that needs to be accounted for in successful self-advocacy. The goal is to help students view the primary focus on the organization's goals as a neutral factor that must be addressed, rather than as a negative or a personal response directed at them.

Students may find thinking about Phil's goals as a new experience. They often cannot understand how Teresa or Jessie can help Phil. Some youth may even feel that Phil has a moral or legal obligation to provide Teresa or Jessie with a job.

Students will recognize that Phil has the power associated with being a boss. It is often assumed he is not open to anything that will help Jessie or Teresa despite any effort to demonstrate how their work can benefit the bakery. This can be an enjoyable exercise as students begin to realize that Teresa and Jessie have some power as a result of their abilities to advance Phil's objectives.

Another difficult concept for students to understand is that Phil may not know how Teresa or Jessie can support the bakery's objectives unless they explain it to him. A successful self-advocate must recognize that even the boss may not be aware of all information or have all the solutions to a challenging situation. Presenting **solutions** in self-advocacy is a critical component that must be reinforced.

There are only a few stated facts in this exercise. Yet students will have plenty to analyze in terms of discovering Phil's specific goals, as well as ways Teresa and Jessie can support those goals. The ability to analyze the other's goals must be developed to become an effective self-advocate.

Case Discussion

Review Case #8 and the questions in the student casebook.

Below are some important questions to consider if not already discussed.

Does an employer always have the ability, the need, and the time to focus on the employee's needs?

- Never assume that people in charge will understand how your goals meet their purposes. You usually won't even get their attention unless you first focus on their goals.

- A good employer and employee relationship is one in which both parties' needs and goals are served. This is referred to as **complementary** needs and objectives. At times, the employee may have a responsibility to demonstrate this relationship to get support for his or her own goals.

- Often an employee has a wide range of personal objectives and strengths that can support an employer's goals.

How can pursuing your present personal goals be beneficial for an organization?

- Carefully analyze the goals and needs of an organization and determine how you can support those goals in exchange for support for your personal goals.

Which of Teresa's strengths would be most useful for Phil's bakery?

- She has known the business for four months. If she leaves, Phil would have the expense of hiring and training a replacement who might not work out as well as Teresa.

- She has ambition and motivation to learn new skills (bookkeeping) that help the bakery.

- She enjoys people, and the bakery is dependent upon good relationships.

- She could use her ambition to help Phil discover new ways to expand his business.

Why might Phil not understand that Teresa and Jessie could help his business make a profit?

- Phil might think Teresa's and Jessie's goals will cost him more money.

- Decision-makers often resist making decisions unless they are forced to or see a clear benefit.

- Even though Phil is the boss, he might be unaware or overlook an employee's talents and commitment to work because his own responsibilities keep him so busy.

What are some personal needs of people in positions of authority and responsibility?

- Want to feel that they are successful

- Want to be appreciated

- Want to be involved with activities that solve problems and promote their organization's mission

- Want to work on things that bring success

- Want to feel that they are positive and helpful

- Want to believe that they are important for their organization's success

How do people communicate their strengths to others?

Ask the students to think of a teacher they like. Do they know all of his or her strengths?

If they know some strengths, demonstrate how that helps them appreciate the teacher.

Then ask students how they came to know these strengths. It could be from the teacher, other students, or other teachers. Ask students to think about how knowing these strengths helped them appreciate the teacher more.

Point out that it takes a good deal of time to discover the person's strengths.

From this discussion, emphasize the following:

- In most self-advocacy situations, the other party does not know your strengths or does not remember them. It is **your** responsibility to communicate your strengths.

- Self-advocates need to create an inventory of their strengths and periodically update this inventory.

- Modesty is a virtue, but communicating strengths **related** to achieving a goal is essential for helping a decision-maker support your self-advocacy goals.

- Strengths include skills, knowledge, achievements, well-developed personal goals, personal values, and experiences of overcoming obstacles.

Role-Play

Ask the class to select the best person to be hired as a sous chef (assistant cook) for a small new restaurant.

Yukiko has worked as a waitress in three different restaurants. The last restaurant was a very high-pressured, high-priced restaurant in midtown Manhattan. Since she was five years old, Yukiko has enjoyed cooking and has learned to make many different cakes and pastries.

Bernie graduated in the top 20 percent of his high school class. He then got a job as a mechanic's assistant fixing trucks. Bernie gets along with many different people and doesn't get upset in high-pressure situations. Bernie is known for throwing great parties and making very complicated meals.

Ask the class to select the best person to receive a scholarship to study transportation engineering.

Fiam has graduated high school and lives with a roommate in Brooklyn. He reports that he has had a very difficult time in school because he was always picked on. He needs the scholarship because he doesn't have enough money.

Stacy dresses very well and has an easy time talking with others. She reports that she had a very stressful childhood. Her parents had extremely difficult times and often she had to live with other relatives and spend some time in foster care.

Ask the students to discuss their reasons for their selections and rejections.

- For the pastry chef, we have learned enough about the strengths of the two individuals to make some judgment about who might be more useful. Yukiko has some related experiences to baking and the restaurant business. Even Bernie has some valuable strengths that might help as a pastry chef. Both might be suitable for the position.

- In the second situation, Fiam and Stacy stress problems rather than strengths. So far, they have given us no information indicating a scholarship would likely result in their success in the transportation engineering field. For example, Fiam did not report that he did very well in math courses and did a major report about transportation systems for a social studies class. Finally, he did not explain how he approaches every task with a great deal of precision.

- Stacy did not explain that growing up, she spent much time on the subways and buses going to different relatives. She became fascinated with the transportation system and would think of ways to make it more useful for riders. Her uncle, a subway conductor, has explained that most people never see all the work done to build and maintain the subways.

Now that we have learned about Stacy and Fiam's strengths related to transportation, we begin to form a different attitude. A scholarship might likely result in success for either of them.

In all four cases, the individuals had important strengths that would make others want to give them the job or scholarship. In these situations, there is no way for the interviewer to know their strengths unless the individuals directly explain them.

Importance of Your Strengths

Students need to learn that it is easier to help someone who is likely to be successful than to help someone who presents him- or herself as a problem or victim. Most people don't want more problems in their lifes.

An essential element of self-advocacy is communicating your strengths to the "other person." This usually requires that the self-advocate presents his or her accomplishments, skills, and values, as well as their future goals. This helps the other person believe that their support will result in success. Communicating problems often places doubts and resistance in the other person's mind.

Discuss in class the introduction to Chapter 3 in the student casebook, especially the section "Concepts to Consider When Presenting Your Strengths."

Case #9

Identifying Your Strengths

When you want support in reaching a goal, it's very tempting to tell the other side all the problems you're having and all the reasons you deserve help. But while the other side may be sympathetic, they will usually feel they can't do much about your problems. To be an effective self-advocate, you must be able to depersonalize (not take it personally) the response you get and focus on presenting your **strengths** *and how you can advance the goals of the organization.*

Background

Many students in your class learn that the fastest way to get attention is to present their problems. Often they will use this approach in any stressful situation. As a result, they will usually fail to gain support for their goals.

The purpose of this case is to **discover new approaches to earning support for an important goal.** It is important for students to recognize that they have value to others. If students learn to communicate this value, they will get the support they need to achieve some of their goals.

The self-advocacy process also helps to depersonalize requests for support. In this case, James takes Lishone's response personally, gets angry, and retreats before attempting a self-advocacy approach. This case illustrates that personalizing the issue, although natural, hinders James's successful attainment of his goals.

A secondary purpose of the case is to encourage students to think about **budgeting.** Independent life will require managing a budget. They will have little margin for mistakes and could face disastrous results if they do not properly budget for their necessary expenses. Therefore, it is important to introduce the idea of saving for a future goal or preparing a contingency plan.

If you have time, you might have the class engage in a budgeting exercise. Making a budget for their first year of independent living is a great way to begin becoming familiar with actual costs.

Equally important is learning how to organize and structure a complex process such as budgeting. Through this process, students learn to understand and define their goals. A sample budget for discussion follows the discussion section.

Case Discussion

Review Case #9 and the questions in the student casebook.

Following are some important questions to consider if not already discussed.

Strengths
James needs to identify and communicate his strengths. What are they?

- James's knowledge of Hannibal Bookstore, combined with college business classes, would make him valuable to Hannibal's management team.

- James identifies with Hannibal and is involved in important activities, such as the Friday night book readings. Identification with the company is like loyalty, and employers consider it very important in getting effective output from an employee.

- James has demonstrated a long-term commitment and loyalty to Hannibal.

- The cost to raise James's salary would be extremely small compared with the benefits Hannibal Bookstore would receive through his education.

- James's core commitment to reading adds to his effectiveness and commitment in the bookstore environment.

Depersonalization
Why is it important to reduce the personal aspects of a problem?

- Helps you become more rational in planning a strategy and sticking with your long-term objectives

- Reduces the chance that the other person will overreact and become highly resistant to your proposals

Context
Are the conditions and surroundings related to the advocacy important?

- In this case, making the self-advocacy presentation more formal might help focus Lishone on the issue and demonstrate its importance.

What ways could James make the discussion more formal?

- Make an appointment to meet with Lishone.

- Make an effective self-advocacy presentation, including

  - Pointing out that Hannibal Bookstore's and Lishone's goals can be supported through supporting James's request

  - Presenting James's strengths

  - Providing a number of possible solutions

  - Identifying important allies (other staff, customers, professors, etc.)

- Follow up with a written proposal after the oral presentation.

- Avoid discussing personal life.

Goals

What are James's immediate goals?

- Getting a salary increase and going to college

Other Issues

Is Lishone the best person to hear James's presentation?

- Perhaps involving someone with more responsibility for improving Hannibal's success might be better. (Remind students to consider what they learned from Chapter 2, "How Systems and Organizations Work.")

Identify important missing facts not yet revealed:

- James's objective for taking business courses
- Chain of command at Hannibal
- How well James is respected in the Hannibal organization

James's objectives may benefit Hannibal; therefore, he needs to find the right person to present his proposal to and the right context in which to do it. Then if James presents his goals by focusing on how his long-term objective of education will benefit Hannibal, he will get interest from Hannibal.

After James has Hannibal interested in the ways he can support the bookstore's objectives, James could explain the specific facts of how much tuition and books will cost. He can then suggest either an increase in salary or direct payment for his college education. He might suggest a loan that would not have to be paid back if James remained at Hannibal for another 18 months. As an alternative, James might suggest additional salary for running the Friday night book readings. Perhaps he can think of something extra to do to make these programs more successful.

Providing a variety of workable solutions and identifying benefits for Hannibal will help the bookstore appreciate the value of supporting James's educational goals. By combining Hannibal's objectives with his own, James moves the problem from merely one employee's inability to pay all his bills to a means for improving Hannibal's future. In this way, James identifies and describes the problem more as an opportunity for Hannibal than as a problem for James. To which approach is Hannibal most likely to respond?

It is useful to explain to the students that they will see this case again later in the semester. We do this in order to provide the experience of studying the case deeper and seeing how other issues can be explained in the same case.

Activity
Sample Budget: Living Expenses

Ask class members to come up with all budget categories. Explain that they may not incur expenses in all areas at first and may get some supplementary support from family, government services, etc. But eventually, if they get a good job, they will need to plan to pay for most of these expenses.

Savings
   Regular
   Emergencies
   Investment

Food
   Groceries
   Eating out

Housing
   Rent
   Security deposit

Utilities
   Electricity
   Gas
   Telephone

Clothing
   Clothes
   Shoes
   Laundry

Personal care
   Haircut
   Soap, shampoo, body care, etc.

Medical
   Insurance
   Direct payments
   Optometrist
   Dentist

Education
   Vocational training
   College
   Books

Transportation
   Car, including gas, insurance, and
   maintenance
   Public transportation

Household
   Furniture
   Cleaning supplies
   Repairs/maintenance not covered
   by landlord

Entertainment
   Books
   Movies
   Video rental
   Going out to concerts, restau-
   rants, clubs, sporting events, etc.

Gifts

Taxes
   Income
   Sales

Now split up the categories among two or more groups and ask them to make an estimate for Jackie, 21 years old, who lives with a friend (splits rent and some other expenses in half or some proportion), has a job as a floor sander, and goes to college at night. She makes $22,235 a year and her company pays 50 percent of medical insurance.

Exercise #3

Presenting Your Strengths

Never assume that the other person knows or remembers your strengths. You need to let others know about your strengths when you advocate for yourself. Write answers to the following questions and keep them for future use. It's a good idea to review and revise (change and/or add new strengths) your answers every three to six months.

Background

It is important that you ask students to **write out their answers** and that you collect the exercise and make a copy to compare when they do the exercise for homework later in the semester.

Recognizing personal strengths is one of the most important skills to master and concepts to understand. Your students have a wide range of talents and skills that remain unknown to the outside world. Most students mistakenly think that others either are aware of their talents, that it doesn't matter, or that it's not appropriate for them to communicate their strengths. Therefore, reinforcing the importance of this exercise and the importance of communicating their strengths will have instrumental impact on the students' successes long into their futures.

Questions

1. Identify at least three personal strengths:

   (Look over the chapter introduction and see how many of the following personal strengths you can think of.)

   - What are your personal or professional goals?

   - Explain some strong values you have.

   - Identify some positions of responsibility you have had.

   - Think of some specific accomplishments you have achieved.

   - List things you are good at doing.

   - List some of your personality strengths.

   - Identify some of the obstacles you have had to overcome in your life.

   - Identify some difficult problems you have solved.

2. Do you let others know about strengths?

   - In the past, how have you let others (family, friends) know about these strengths and successes?

   - How have you let people in authority (teachers, social workers, bosses, or others) know about these strengths and successes?

3. What is the best way to let people know about your past success?

   - Think of when you first meet a teacher, a job supervisor, or a person who might want to help you. What is the best way to let people know about your strengths and past successes?

4. What personal strengths do you want to develop?

   - When thinking about long-term goals, most people discover there are personal areas they want to develop. Improving specific skills and developing more knowledge and experiences in particular areas are some ways to improve your strengths. What strengths do you want to develop?

Discussion

If students cannot identify their strengths, help them to

- Find out what they are interested in and what they have done in these areas.

- Realize that even ambition is a strength.

- Ask others in the class what they think their strengths are. This is both helpful and motivating.

- Develop a serious appreciation for how important this process is for their future success.

You can also help the discovery process by referring to an individual's strengths in class discussion.

Finally, ask students to think carefully about their strengths and successes. Ask them to do Exercise #3 again as homework. This will give students more time to evaluate their strengths.

Begin Discussion About Chapter 4, "Making Transitions"

Read and discuss the introduction of Chapter 4 in the student casebook.

What are changes you have wanted to make but just couldn't seem to make, such as study more for school, get a job, make better friends, become skilled in some activity, etc.?

Why could you never make those changes?

What advice about making a change would you give to someone else?

Explain the three transition zones to students using the chart on page 53 of their books.

Explain homework

Ask students to read Case #10, *Fabiola: From Change to Transition*. Ask them to assume that Fabiola wants to change her life and become a professional in the computer field. Half the students should answer the questions under Group 1 and the other half should answer the questions under Group 2. While reading the case, ask students to think about what might be the reason Fabiola appears to be having such a hard time moving on in her life.

You might even chart it as follows:

Fabiola	Receptionist	Ms. Robinson
Resists leaving present life	Resist**ed** leaving a past life	Resist**ed** leaving a past life
Confused about what she wants to do	Confused for a limited time	Confused for a limited time
Trying to get information to help **make** a decision	**Making** a new beginning	**Made** a good new beginning

If students are overwhelmed by reading this amount of material, advise them on study skills such as breaking the case up into smaller parts and writing in the margins of their books.

CHAPTER 4

Making Transitions

Central to the lives of most of your students is beginning the process of transitioning to independence. This is one of the more challenging of life's transitions. Self-advocacy, career preparation, academic achievement, and other independent living skills are critical for success. An additional way to help students make successful transitions is to explore the process itself and create understanding for the natural stages and actions one can take to make the transition lasting. Understanding transitions can help a student go beyond making merely a physical change that is not lasting, to a transition that is successful.

Take time with this chapter. "Transitions" is a process we all struggle with and there is as much potential for increasing your own understanding as well as the students'. This makes the process more collaborative and stimulating.

Begin the discussion with the examples of Bernice, Malcolm, and Tiebauld from the introduction of Chapter 4 in the student casebook.

In each these cases the person makes a change and then cannot seem to stick with it. What prevented the person from sticking with this change?

What kind of positive identity does Bernice get from hanging out with friends after work?

- Bernice is most likely well-liked and respected by these friends.

- Bernice probably doesn't get this type of recognition at her job. (She seems to want to move to another job.)

- Bernice probably doesn't have to do much to be liked and respected by her friends.

- These friends are familiar; meeting new friends might produce anxiety.

- Hanging out fits easily into her personal and work schedule.

What benefits does Bernice get from hanging out with her friends?

- She gets respect and friendship.

- She doesn't have to work at gaining friendship.

- Her friendships fit her schedule.

- Her friends keep her from having to deal with the uncertainty of anything new.

Why might she resist not hanging out with her friends?

- Pain of leaving something important and familiar.

- Fear of losing the identity she has from her friends' respect and friendship.

- Fear of being set loose, becoming disconnected.

What will Bernice have to do to stop hanging out with her friends after work so she can do well in college?

- Think about what exactly she will lose by not hanging out.

- Realize that friendships she loses because she can't hang out might not be as strong as she thought they were.

- Consider the change she will have to make—perhaps she can still hang out with these friends one day a week or on weekends.

Should Bernice consider her time spent hanging out a bad period in her life? Why?

- No, it was important for her at the time. Now she has different needs, but that doesn't minimize the importance of her past needs.

How can Bernice honor or show respect for this period of her life?

- If she goes to college, she might suggest a party or special celebration with her friends to mark the end of hanging out every night.

Does Bernice have to end all the relationships she had with the people she hung out with after work?

- No, she can meet some of them at other times.

After the class goes through this exercise, if there is time, they can do the same thing with Malcolm and Tiebauld. Suggest they use the "Making Transitions" chart to help them answer the questions.

Case #10

Transitions

Everyone experiences the transitions process when they make successful and lasting changes. While going through the transitions process is similar, each person does it in a different way. To understand the process, the chart is separated into three zones (stages); however, most people experience being in more than one zone at any one time. In this next case, see if you can find evidence to demonstrate the different zones each character is in and what they do to move through the zone. Remember, any character can be in more than one zone at a time.

Background

Many students can make changes that will help them further their education, get jobs, and even begin to pursue meaningful careers. However, too many students fail to make these changes last. Thus, we have the distinction between *change* and *transition*. In many cases, students instinctively struggle with transition but fail to understand the process. This failure to understand the process results in feelings of failure and frustration that prevent any enduring transition.

If you can help students understand that transition is different from change, and that all successful individuals go through such a process, it will help your students make lasting transitions.

This chapter includes only one long case. The case reinforces transitions ideas and demonstrates how all successful individuals must engage in transitions to take meaningful steps toward reaching their long-term goals.

The case revolves around an informational interview. This will reinforce the informational interview process. The informational interview is in the neutral zone, when a student is creatively exploring paths to new beginnings. The informational interview will be most effective for students deeply engaged in the process of endings. These students will be most able to handle the creative nature of getting information about prospective careers.

Case Discussion

After the students read and discuss the chapter, go through the "Making Transitions" chart. Demonstrate how the chart will be useful for a quick reference to transition theory, will provide tools for getting through each transition zone, and can serve as a valuable guide for analyzing the case.

Finally, you can go through the case paragraph by paragraph with the class and use the narrative to explore transitions theory and methods for successfully moving through each zone.

The following is the case marked up to indicate the different transition zones. It is a model of how students should mark up their own case copies.

<u>Underline</u> represents examples of the **endings** zone.

Bold represents examples of the **neutral** zone.

Italic represents examples of the **new beginnings** zone.

Below is an analysis for each paragraph that you may use for the class discussion.

1. At 8:19 a.m., Fabiola found herself on Fifth Avenue and 59th Street in New York City. The neighborhood was unfamiliar. People were hurrying in and out of a white skyscraper over 55 stories high. Fabiola checked an address scribbled on a card. It matched that of the skyscraper, but Fabiola <u>walked away.</u> **Why was she here?** She had an appointment for an informational interview with a computer security company.

2. <u>This appointment frightened her.</u> **What was the point?** She had graduated high school two years ago. **She had had three different jobs since then.** After graduation she worked at servicing computers at a large advertising company. The job was not interesting. All she did was plug in computers. She was promised a promotion, but when the company had financial troubles, Fabiola was the first to be let go. It took three months to get her next job at a messenger service.

3. At the messenger service, Fabiola worked as an expediter, arranging for the deliveries of packages. She quit this job because it was boring. She now works as a sales clerk in a clothing store. **<u>This job doesn't excite her either.</u>** She likes clothes but hates helping rude customers. Three months ago, she moved out of her mother's apartment into her own apartment. The situation at home was really bad and she had to get out.

4. With only 11 minutes before her scheduled appointment, Fabiola was now more than a block away and walking in the wrong direction. Fabiola was *thinking she had made a mistake,* a big mistake, in leaving home.

5. Could it be that it hadn't been so bad when she lived at home? She remembers hating living at home. Now she felt differently. This change in her thinking added to her confusion. She didn't have high rent to pay when she lived with her mother. She had lots of friends. Often she was able to save money to go to some clubs and buy great clothes. But now that she was independent, Fabiola was struggling to pay her bills. <u>Independence seemed to require more than just moving out.</u>

6. If she made her appointment today, this would be her fifth informational interview. She remembered her feelings when she was fired from the advertising company. For months <u>she felt anxious and angry with everyone.</u> She never wanted to feel that way again. Even though her present job was nothing great, she was hesitant to try anything different. Someone had told her that if she wanted to get far in computers, she would either have to go to college or take some advanced computer training. <u>Fabiola did not like the idea of being a student again.</u>

7. Fabiola watched the people on the street. They seemed important. She watched a truck go by. Its sign read "Computer Services." Fabiola wondered about the kinds of jobs they were heading to. She heard a different voice inside her head. It told her **to turn around** and go to her informational interview. She had five minutes to be on time.

8. Fabiola stopped and looked back at the full height of the white skyscraper. Everything seemed confusing. She would like to work with computers, but she also thought **her life was a failure and she was too far behind.** She thought about all the people streaming into the building. They seemed to have **a purpose. What was hers?**

9. Fabiola entered the white skyscraper. The entrance ceiling was three or four stories high. Well-dressed security guards stood behind marble counters. There were lines of people in front of each security person. Everyone was in a hurry to get where they were going. Fabiola waited in a line. When it was her turn, the security guard asked her where she was going. "Janet Robinson, Security Designs." The guard called to confirm Fabiola's appointment. "Take the third elevator to the 44th floor."

10. The elevator raced to the 44th floor. Fabiola found herself in a large reception area. She was impressed with the three large sofas and a beautiful wooden table with magazines on it. The receptionist was a young man. He wore a suit and tie. He seemed very professional. He asked Fabiola who she was here to see. "Janet Robinson, I have an 8:30 appointment. My name is Fabiola Lewison."

11. "Have a seat, Ms. Lewison. I'll tell Ms. Robinson you're here. Would you like some coffee or water?"

12. Fabiola sat on a beautiful white sofa. She had *little experience with anyone calling her "Ms. Lewison" with respect.* Fabiola thought the receptionist had confused her with someone else. She was so confused she didn't reply to the receptionist's offer. The same thought came back to her, **"What's the use?** When the receptionist leaves his desk, I'll get out of here fast."

13. **Maybe** her <u>present job as a sales clerk in the clothing store was not so bad.</u> Fabiola knew everyone who worked at the store and she had a number of friends. Other clerks thought she was funny. If she stayed another four months, she would get a raise. Maybe she could afford her studio apartment if she offered to share it with a friend. The work wasn't all that hard and she liked the hours—1:00 p.m. to 8:30 p.m. She didn't have to wake up early. **What was the point of trying something harder and more demanding?** <u>She would probably fail, and then she would really be mad at herself.</u>

14. **Waiting for Ms. Robinson gave Fabiola time to think about her life. She was confused because her past always seemed to be a bit different whenever she thought about it.** In the past, things had always seemed rough for Fabiola. Her family had very little money and needed help from relatives and sometimes the government. Her mother suffered depression when her first marriage broke up and used drugs for a number of years. During that time, Fabiola

was placed in foster care. She was 16. Fabiola remained in foster care until she was 19. She was placed in two different group homes and transferred to three different high schools.

15. Fabiola was fortunate to be able to leave the foster care system at 19 and return to her home. Yet, she remembers being scared about leaving foster care. But when she returned home, it was different. Her mother no longer used drugs and was not as depressed. Her mother had married another man with whom she had two children.

16. Even though Fabiola had moved home, she rarely saw her mother or stepfather. Her mother worked late into the night and her stepfather had two jobs. They seemed to care about Fabiola but never had time for her. When Fabiola moved home, she had to look after her younger stepbrother and stepsister. This took a lot of time. Sometimes she even thought foster care was easier. All this made Fabiola more confused.

17. Fabiola picked up a magazine about computers. The receptionist was answering phone calls. **Fabiola thought of herself as smart, but now things seemed to make no sense.** She continued to think about her past. Fabiola's stepfather and mother had little time to help Fabiola understand her own strengths. In foster care no one told her she was good at anything. They always seemed more concerned with her problems. At school Fabiola never got good grades, although a few teachers told her she was smart and had "promise." But no one ever told her what to do with "promise."

18. Fabiola's experiences with being on her own had given her great strengths, but Fabiola really had no idea how she could use them to become successful and reach some of her dreams. She had taken **a self-advocacy seminar** and learned how to use informational interviews to gain knowledge about the opportunities that were out there. She had already done four of these interviews. The last interviewer helped her set up this meeting.

19. <u>She had had a tough home life, but she was beginning to think it was a mistake to leave it so soon.</u> Her younger stepbrother and stepsister were family and loved her, and even her stepfather could be fun. Maybe it hadn't been all that bad.

20. **Thoughts whirled through her head:** too many jobs, too many ideas about what she should do with her life, and too many regrets about leaving her family and other jobs. Maybe she should go back home, help her mother with the younger children, and wait until she was more ready to be on her own. *Maybe this informational interview would help her find the answer.*

21. Fabiola stared at the receptionist. There was a pause in phone calls and he noticed her stare. He said, "None of my friends or family believe it. At this time two years ago, I was nowhere. **Nothing mattered then.**"

22. The receptionist walked to a window and pointed outside. "Trouble was all around me then. I was in high school. Everyone was on my case. Teachers, guidance counselors, social workers, and especially the assistant principal. <u>Fought them all. No one was going to push me around.</u> Spent so much time fighting, I never did schoolwork or thought of my future."

23. Fabiola didn't know what to say, and for a long time the receptionist just looked out the window in silence. He continued, **"I didn't do anything for a year after I graduated.** Finally, I realized <u>I missed high school!</u> Strange. Just couldn't get going until I realized that high school life was over."

24. The receptionist walked back to his desk. "Now I have a job. *I'll be a fraud investigator in four years.* I have a job that pays the bills."

25. The receptionist answered a call. After hanging up the phone, he asked Fabiola to come with him. Fabiola did not know why, but she followed the receptionist rather than catch the next elevator to freedom.

26. They went down a hallway into a large room with many cubicles. Each cubicle had computers. Some cubicles were empty, others had a number of people looking at the screens, and many had just one person working on a computer.

27. The receptionist led Fabiola to one of the cubicles. A woman wearing a blue suit and white blouse was standing in front of the cubicle and explaining something to a group of people. When the woman wearing the white blouse saw Fabiola, she told the group they would have to meet later. She suggested to Fabiola that they go to the conference room. Fabiola felt a wave of excitement at seeing all these professionals working with computers.

28. Fabiola was stunned by the time they reached the conference room. Everything was happening fast. Would she be able to say anything? She remembered advice from the self-advocacy seminar and took out her agenda.

29. "I'm a bit nervous, excuse me." Fabiola decided to just begin at the beginning of her agenda. "I am very pleased that you have time for me. My goal is to have a career in computer security. Mr. Hightower told me that you started Security Designs. He told me that you are very experienced in computer security. I want to work in the field of information security. Your advice would be extremely useful."

30. Ms. Robinson asked Fabiola to talk a little about her interests and her background. Fabiola explained her interests in computer security and tried to communicate her strengths. Ms. Robinson was very serious. Fabiola wasn't sure if Ms. Robinson was interested in her.

31. Ms. Robinson asked Fabiola why she had so many jobs lately. Unfortunately, Fabiola had not planned a response to this obvious question. "Well… guess I was having a **hard time finding myself.**" This honest response encouraged Ms. Robinson to talk about her own life.

32. For eight years, Ms. Robinson had worked for an accounting firm. She became their best computer expert. Everyone treated her with respect. Her boss gave her bonuses and sent her on exciting trips. Yet, Ms. Robinson felt her **work had no purpose.** She did not like working alone. She started to think about opening her own company, but she was afraid. She <u>feared giving up everyone's respect</u> and her <u>high salary.</u> She was good at her work but <u>was afraid she would not have the skills to manage her own company.</u>

33. Ms. Robinson had realized that her life as a computer expert was good, but it was not what she wanted. She had to end this chapter. Yet after she quit her job, she thought she had made a <u>horrible mistake.</u> She got a few <u>temporary jobs to support herself. She was worried and dazed. She talked</u> with many people in the computer, accounting, and finance fields. She got different ideas for starting a business, but none of them seemed right. She thought about **giving up computer work and becoming an actress.**

34. A young woman politely interrupted them and asked Ms. Robinson if she could submit a quotation to a client for a year of security work. Ms. Robinson looked at the quotation. She noted that intrusion detection had been left out. Fabiola didn't understand all these new terms, but she was enjoying herself. Ms. Robinson's story had an effect on her. She did not feel as alone.

35. Ms. Robinson picked up her story. For four months, she was **so confused that she hardly worked or left home.** She continued to feel she had made a <u>horrible mistake.</u> During the end of that four-month period, Ms. Robinson *began to realize how much she wanted to investigate security breaches.* She joined the Computer Security Institute and read everything about computer security. *She learned that this type of work would allow her to meet more people.* Finally, she used the advice she had been given and all that she had read to *develop a plan for how she could reach her goals.*

36. "I know you didn't want to hear my life story. But I want you to know that we all struggle to reach our dreams. My advice: *Start thinking of yourself as an information specialist.* Once you start *seeing yourself differently, things will be easier.* <u>What you have done is great, but now you are ready to move on.</u>"

37. The meeting stretched to an hour. Fabiola met some computer specialists and saw the work they did. Her sense of confusion was losing out to excitement. At the end of the meeting, Ms. Robinson suggested that with the information Fabiola was gathering she should begin to develop a plan. She also urged her to accept what she had already done in her life but move on to a new beginning. Ms. Robinson hinted that she might be willing to help Fabiola find a job or internship when she was ready.

Transitions Case Analysis

It is useful to review this analysis before class. It will help students gain more understanding from this case.

Paragraph 1

The informational interview is a potential gateway to a new beginning. However, Fabiola is having difficulty. She literally turns around and walks back toward her present life. Today Fabiola must move from her past to something unfamiliar. Her difficulty in doing this relates to the pain of losing something familiar. If she can make an ending and identify and confront the loss, she will increase her ability to make a permanent change.

Making an ending will be the most difficult concept for students to understand and incorporate into their own actions. While students may have less resistance to the idea that endings are essential for new beginnings, most will resist the idea that endings involve significant struggles. Therefore, it is useful to explore all the facts related to Fabiola's resistance to endings, analyze the difficulties she encounters, and lead discussions related to the "Making Transitions" chart about ways Fabiola can help herself get through these endings.

Perhaps Fabiola is trying to understand the reasons for making the ending when she asks herself the question "Why was she here?" Trying to understand the reasons for making an ending is a useful tool in confronting her ending. The question "Why was she here?" also indicates a position in the neutral zone.

The informational interview in many ways symbolizes presence in the neutral zone. It is a time when people prepare for new beginnings by creatively exploring all paths to such beginnings. It is also a time of confusion and a feeling of loss of purpose. The informational interview is a specific action taken to work through the neutral zone. This might be a good time to review the purpose of the informational interview.

Paragraph 2

Even though Fabiola demonstrates fear about the informational interview, this fear may be more related to resisting leaving her present life. Endings are frightening because they symbolize movement to a new identity. Fabiola is a smart woman, and it is natural for her to possess these feelings. It is useful that Fabiola begins to go over her past job situation. Eventually this will help her understand the reasons why she is making the ending.

By Fabiola asking "What was the point?" she indicates she is in both the endings and neutral zones. In the process of trying to answer this question, Fabiola will more clearly understand why she needs to make this ending. At the same time, her confusion indicates she is already in the neutral zone. This confusion is likely to lead to a creative process in transitioning to a beneficial new beginning.

"What was the point?" also means that Fabiola may have lost the understanding of her life's purpose. No clear purpose and three jobs in a short time certainly indicate that she is presently in the neutral zone.

Having made the appointment for the informational interview represents a move toward a new beginning.

This might be a good time to lead a discussion about why leaving the life associated with high school is difficult to do. What do students think will be different after high school? What will they miss the most? Is there anything they don't like about high school life now that they can see missing in a few years? Are there things they will be forced to do and make decisions about after they leave high school that they may not want to face? Will their present identities become different when they leave high school? Are they identities they don't want to give up? How do they feel about being forced to leave high school rather than choosing their own time?

Try to get students to understand that there will be a major shift in their lives when leaving high school and that it is natural to struggle with this change and resist the ending. Do they know any adults who have never really left their high school period of life? How does this affect them as adults?

Paragraph 3

Fabiola keeps changing jobs but remains uninterested and uninvolved. Even though she wants to work, nothing excites her and she is disenchanted. This is a sign that she is beginning to make the necessary ending. She is most likely disoriented, too. A sense that her life is going somewhere is breaking down.

Note that Fabiola is quite capable of change. Changing jobs and moving out of her home are both big changes. Yet change is different from transition. Because she hasn't gone through the ending process, she cannot make a transition, and any change she makes will most likely not last or be a meaningful progression in Fabiola's life.

Paragraph 4

Fabiola's continued resistance to going to her appointment, along with feelings that she "had made a big mistake," is evidence that she is struggling with making an ending. While Fabiola is still walking away, she is appropriately dealing with issues common to the endings zone, which will help her eventually to make a transition. Again, she is learning that she can view her life in a new way from different vantage points. This is critical for becoming receptive to new views of her future. If she can make an ending with her present situation, she can become a new person.

Paragraph 5

The process of thinking about one's life or writing an autobiography is a useful tool for moving through the neutral zone. To prosper in the neutral zone, Fabiola needs to learn that the past can have different meanings from different perspectives and times in her life. Her doubts about how she had once perceived her past are indictors that she is in the neutral zone. It is useful that she is discovering her perceptions can change. This will help her understand that the present may not be the way she is thinking about it either. If she can let go of her conceptions of the present, it will make it easier for her to conceive a new future. Fabiola may now be ready to see herself as a different person. What once worked in the past may not work anymore. That doesn't mean the past was bad, just that things are now different.

Paragraph 6

Some endings Fabiola experienced were unwilling. When she was forced out of the advertising agency, she was angry and anxious. Even though she now has a new job, Fabiola has not made an ending with her present life and thinking. This is probably the reason she moves from job to job without any satisfaction or feeling that she is moving ahead.

A challenge with endings is giving up an old identity and accepting a new identity. Fabiola's resistance to being a student is a hard part of making an ending. Becoming a student at this point in her life may seem like slipping backward. Because Fabiola would be an older student, she would need to have a different perspective. She may be confused about this new identify.

This is a good point to lead a discussion about useful tools Fabiola could use to help her make an ending with her present life. Go through each step in the "Making Transitions" chart.

What might Fabiola lose by making this ending?

- Relaxed lifestyle with reduced responsibilities

- Little risk of failure

- No urgency to struggle to gain larger life goals

- Comfortable social life

- Freedom to move from job to job as soon as she loses interest

- No need to learn new skills or knowledge for her work

What reasons might Fabiola have for making an ending with her present life?

- She cannot accept new challenges and reach new goals unless she gives up a life with little responsibility.

- With increasing responsibility and goal-setting, she needs to give up a life that does not include future planning.

- To reach new goals, Fabiola must give up the part of her self-image that still views herself as a high school student without adult strengths.

What changes will Fabiola have to make in her behavior and attitudes?

- Fabiola will need to focus on and plan for long-term goals rather than satisfy her immediate desires.

- Fabiola may have to structure her life to devote some time to school or training in order to reach long-term career goals. This may entail giving up some of her social life and sticking with a boring job if it pays the bills.

How should Fabiola treat her past?

- She must recognize that the lifestyle she has been living was good for her. It gave her a chance to experiment with her feelings and develop ideas about who she is. She should not think she wasted any time; rather, she wouldn't be prepared to move into a more focused life if she had not lived the life she had.

- If Fabiola does eventually decide to go into computer work and does decide to get training or go to college, she might consider having a party or going out with a few friends to announce this decision and celebrate her past and her departure from it.

Paragraph 7

It is normal while in the neutral zone to be confused. Turning around and being uncertain about a decision is the norm.

Paragraph 8

Fabiola is envious of others who may sense a purpose in their lives. At the moment, she feels as if she doesn't have a purpose in her life, that her life is a failure. This is common in the neutral zone. She should not feel nervous about an undefined purpose. This is natural for the neutral zone, and being in the neutral zone will eventually help her creatively explore paths to new beginnings.

Paragraph 12

Here Fabiola is beginning to experience a new identity. She feels like a new and different person just in the way she is treated. She is gaining new understandings and attitudes about herself, which is a sign she is entering the new beginnings zone.

Fabiola is unsure of her purpose. "What's the use?" is a common feeling in the neutral zone.

Paragraph 13

This is a great example of how in the same thought someone can be in two transition zones, as in this case, the neutral and endings zones. "Maybe" demonstrates confusion. This confusion and uncertainty are not to be resisted but rather used as a sign that Fabiola is struggling to make a transition and give herself the opportunity to linger in the neutral zone long enough to be creative in finding a suitable new beginning.

In the same thought about her present job, it appears that Fabiola is reluctant to let go and make an ending. While it is clear that Fabiola knows her last series of jobs is taking her nowhere, she is afraid to move on. She is afraid of admitting that maybe she made a mistake when she had decided to get jobs solely for the purpose of leaving home. Therefore, she wants to find a reason not to make an ending: "Maybe her present job was not so bad." This challenge is all associated with making a real ending.

Usually, whenever people question the "point" of something, it is an indication they are in the neutral zone, where life has lost its purpose. At the same time, if they question the point, it gives them the opportunity to explore many paths to a new beginning. Thus, questioning the point can be very useful.

Note that while Fabiola is obviously within the neutral zone, she still needs to engage in and complete the process of ending. She isn't quite there yet, as she continues to fear failure.

Paragraph 14

When Fabiola recognizes that the past can appear different from different points in her life, she is experiencing an important perception associated with being in the neutral zone. Again, this is an extremely important perception. It helps people realize that what they think is factual actually changes with time and perspective. It helps them recognize that they are open to changing their thinking, and this allows them to be creative and think of a wide range of new beginnings, even if they may seem implausible at the moment.

Paragraphs 15–17

Fabiola's thoughts about her past personal story are an important tool to use while in the neutral zone. By going over the past, new goals can be discovered. Fabiola had difficult and good times in her past. In going over her life, she can see more clearly what she feels is still missing and develop goals in those directions. While in the neutral zone, it is useful to spend some time alone. Even though Fabiola sits in the reception area with the receptionist, she has some moments to think alone. She probably needs to spend even greater periods alone.

Paragraph 17

When things make no sense for Fabiola, she is in the neutral zone. When something makes no sense, there is greater chance for creativity. With this creativity, there is a greater chance for a successful new beginning.

Paragraph 18

Fabiola needs to use her time in the neutral zone to discover what she really wants and to identify what she would miss if she does not make an ending.

Paragraph 20

Whirling thoughts can be overwhelming, but they also can lead people to break away from their usual thinking and to be creative. Spending time in the neutral zone is very important and useful. It is apparent that Fabiola is moving toward becoming a new person. She is engaged in the entire transition process and is even venturing into the new beginnings zone. This is the time for something important, and it indicates a new understanding and a new identity for her.

Paragraph 21

Now the receptionist is relating a transition experience. He begins by talking about his presence in the neutral zone when nothing mattered.

Paragraph 22

Rather than move on when he finished high school, the receptionist clearly had a hard time adjusting to leaving his teenage identity. His anger, which may have been from other causes unknown to us, was expressed in his resistance to moving forward. He decided to fight rather than come up with a path to a new beginning. He was blocked and did not deal with making an ending.

Paragraph 23

It was extremely hard for the receptionist to make an ending with the life associated with his late teens. Also, he wandered in the neutral zone for a long time.

Paragraph 31

Fabiola admits to being in the neutral zone, which is indication to herself and to Ms. Robinson that she is closer to the new beginnings zone than the endings zone.

Paragraph 32

Now Ms. Robinson also relates a transition story. She talks about the time she spent in the endings zone. Pain and difficulty can be expressed in boredom. Ms. Robinson still remembers being afraid, fearing an identity loss, and worrying she would lose something familiar. Notice how the neutral zone and endings zone overlap again. Perhaps being in the neutral zone for Ms. Robinson precipitated her moving into and through the endings zone.

Paragraph 33

It is common to be afraid of making a mistake when going through an ending and trying to separate from the past. There are two different levels of mistakes. The mistake she refers to is leaving her job. But the other mistake Ms. Robinson might begin to sense is that of selecting her first job, which she initially thought was so great. By leaving the job, she felt as though she was acknowledging that she had made a mistake in the first place. Of course this is not true, since her perspective changed after she had worked at her first job for some time.

Ms. Robinson remembered feeling worried and confused. Her neutral zone appears to have been intensely difficult, but it also appears to have provided the creativity to formulate a great new beginning.

Paragraph 35

The neutral zone's creative nature, combined with an opportunity to explore new paths, allowed Ms. Robinson to develop a great new beginning. She appears to have gained new understandings, values, attitudes, and identity. She also worked hard to use information to develop a plan for reaching her goals.

Paragraphs 36 and 37

At the end of the meeting, Ms. Robinson gave Fabiola good advice. If she wants to move on, Fabiola should begin to think of herself as a different person. This is important for reaching that new beginning. Another great piece of advice was for Fabiola to respect her past, which will help her separate from the endings zone.

CHAPTER 5

Finding Mentors and Allies

Many of your students will have a limited idea about the mentoring relationship. Thus, it is important to develop understanding of the following three concepts:

1. Critical to successful mentoring is understanding that it is a dynamic and reciprocal relationship. While the mentor may play the role of a coach or teacher, the "mentoree" has equally important roles to play to make the relationship successful. Therefore, understanding why someone would want to be a mentor is of critical importance.

2. Because mentoring revolves around a relationship, a student must be proactive in recruiting a mentor.

3. Finally, the need for a mentor is not the exclusive province of a teenager or someone from a challenging background. All successful people, throughout their lives, rely on others who can provide mentoring advice and facilitate understanding.

Case #11

Identifying Potential Mentors and Allies

When you develop new goals or want to try something different, a mentor and or an ally can be extremely useful. This is true at any age and for any occupation. The successful self-advocate identifies people who could be useful mentors and effective allies.

Background

The idea of using mentors and allies throughout life is not readily apparent to most students. They have come to believe such relationships are only necessary when they are just beginning in life.

This case is about spotting potential mentors and then figuring out ways to engage their assistance. David is very fortunate because he has met Hilary and Stone who are in a position to give advice and, with some good advocacy, might help finance David's new company. Hilary, Stone, and David's wife's boss can be instrumental in helping develop a good business plan that might result in some financing. Finally, his craftspeople friends can be very helpful in providing information about costs and the time to do certain jobs, as well as operating as a source of good workers for his company.

If David recognizes the value of good mentoring and finds a way to enlist the support of all his potential mentors, he can be very successful. Hopefully, this case can help motivate students to begin to take advantage of mentors in their present situations.

Case Discussion

Review Case #11 and the questions from the student casebook.

Following are some important questions to consider if not already discussed.

Why would someone at David's age and with his experience need a mentor?

- David has learned a great deal about plumbing. However, he hasn't had much experience running his own business. Other people who have been successful at business and making money could provide valuable advice from their experiences. This advice could save David a great amount of time as well as increase his chances of success at beginning his own business.

- David knows the plumbing trade but doesn't have much knowledge of the details of the other trades. People with experience from other trades could provide David with very useful advice and information about budgeting and job complexity. This could be of great help in estimating jobs and getting them done properly.

Why would David's potential mentors want to provide advice and knowledge to him?

- Hilary and Stone might want to invest in David's new company to make money. Therefore, they would most likely be willing to offer help in building David's company. They also might want to contribute their expertise to a person they have come to respect.

- David's wife's boss might want to help David because he respects and values David's wife's work. He can help David's wife by helping David at little cost, and he may enjoy helping a competent person succeed in business. Finally, he knows that as David's business succeeds, David will become a great resource for new business.

- The other trades people might want to help David because it might turn into more business for them and because over the years, they have gained respect for David and want to see him succeed.

David has graduated from college and learned about business plans and financing. Why should he need anyone else's advice or knowledge?

- Actual experience can be very useful and supplement academic knowledge one learns at school.

- These potential mentors have a keen interest in David's success and thus are likely to give him extensive support he wouldn't get from anyone else.

- As David begins his business, he can go back to these mentors for additional advice and information.

- They can be important psychological support during the process of building his business.

Case #12

Establishing a Mentorship

All successful people have mentors. Most people have different mentors at different times in their lives. Successful people know how to develop mentoring relationships. In some cultures and situations, mentors are assigned to people. Yet many of us need to search out our own mentors.

Background

Many young adults have heard about mentors, and some understand the importance of having a mentoring relationship with someone who has more experience. What most young adults don't know is that a useful mentoring relationship has a great deal to do with their part in the relationship. Understanding the mentor's needs is just as important as understanding the needs of an employer or anyone else with whom the students will have some transactional relationship.

Case Discussion

Review Case #12 and the questions from the student casebook.

Following are some important questions to consider if not already discussed.

Are mentors only useful for students?

- All successful people have mentors. Most people have different mentors at different times throughout their lives. Successful people know how to develop mentoring relationships. In some cultures and situations, mentors are assigned to people, but most of us need to search out our own mentors.

What reasons might someone have for being a mentor?

- Desire to teach, coach, and help
- Desire to learn more about a subject
- Potential to get some help from the person being mentored
- Desire to pass on experience that one has learned
- Desire to help someone who is experiencing similar challenges in his or her life

Why does Jasda need mentoring from Ms. Greer?

- Saves Jasda from making costly mistakes in seeking his goals
- Teaches Jasda about opportunities of which he is unaware
- Helps Jasda develop a stronger relationship with a potential ally

What reasons might Ms. Greer have to mentor Jasda?

- Ms. Greer understands what it is like to have challenges in one's life.

- Ms. Greer is very serious and dedicated to her work and might welcome helping someone who is equally serious and wants to contribute to the job.

What advice would you give Jasda for building a mentoring relationship with Ms. Greer?

- Jasda needs to communicate that he is highly motivated and wants to advance his career in shipping.

- Jasda should demonstrate appreciation to anyone who can help him gain more information and advice on how to advance his career.

- Jasda needs to communicate to Ms. Greer exactly how he has used the information and advice she has given to him.

CHAPTER 6

Depersonalizing Issues and Recognizing the Needs of Others

Successful self-advocacy requires two emotional transitions from common adolescent behavior. It is your challenge to help students understand the importance of the following:

1. **Depersonalizing Issues.** Students need to understand that creating solutions to problems require a focus on the challenge and solution rather than on the personality of the other person. A successful self-advocate will be more effective if he or she can focus on rational presentations rather than judging and often misjudging the personal likes and dislikes of the other person.

2. **Recognizing the Needs of Others.** Students need to understand that in any successful negotiation or self-advocacy, all parties must gain something. Thus, it is critical to understand the needs of the other party. This is another challenge for adolescents and therefore requires useful analysis and discussions to create understanding.

Case #13

Depersonalizing Issues and Analyzing the Needs of Others

Often when you need something from an organization, you have to deal with a supervisor. This can be frustrating when the supervisor (other person) seems to have a lot on his or her mind and doesn't appear to care about what you want to say. Trying to understand what the other person is concerned about can help you reach your goals.

Background

One of the reasons to learn self-advocacy is to help depersonalize issues. Negotiations, advocacy, or any kind of communication attempting to change the opinion of another or seek their support is more effective when the personal element is removed.

Students are at a stage where they view most actions by others as personal. If someone does something supportive, it is "because they like me." If someone does something contrary to their needs, it is "because they don't like me." Both assumptions lead to reactions that usually do not help students to think about what the real issues are, what needs others have, and how they can plan their response to gain continued support for their needs.

Case Discussion

Review Case #13 and the questions from the student casebook.

See Case #6 for a breakdown of facts.

Following are some important questions to consider if not already discussed.

Who do you think was justified to be angry in this case? Nat? Harnett? Alicia? Alicia's mother? Tanya? Danielle?

What if Alicia had said, "...Look Nat, I'm busy now. I really don't have time to get anyone to cover for your lunch hour because you gave me such late notice. Do you think you could stay through lunch and work until 3:00 p.m. and then take the rest of the day off to help your friend?"

Do you think Nat would have been satisfied?

- He would probably be satisfied because this would give him an extra hour off, and if it took longer to help his friend, he wouldn't have to return to work. Harnett should probably be able to delay his discharge from the hospital for a couple hours.

- He should be satisfied because this is a good deal.

If the above is a reasonable solution, how could Nat have been effective in his self-advocacy if he had not allowed his anger to control his actions?

- He could have waited until Alicia was not overstressed and admitted he made a mistake in not asking sooner.

Case #14

Connecting Your Goals with the Needs of the Organization

In evaluating whether to support your proposal, the other person will evaluate how it supports the needs and goals of his or her organization and how well suited you are to succeed if you are given the support.

Background

Effective self-advocates need to demonstrate that if an organization supports their goals and objectives, it will also support the organization's goals. Students have a tendency to make proposals based solely on their needs and objectives. When a student's proposed initiative might support the organization's goals, the student too often fails to recognize this benefit or communicate it to the organization. Even when a student does recognize a benefit to the organization, he or she will often assume it is apparent and find no need to communicate the benefit.

This is another opportunity to discuss budgeting and review some expenses and income needs students will have when they reach independence. In this case, such a budget is presented in a relevant context. You might spend some time talking about the budget and exploring its accuracy.

Case Discussion

Review Case #14 and the questions from the student casebook.

Explain how James's continued loyalty to Hannibal and his studying business management would benefit Hannibal.

- James has been a clerk for seven months and is valuable because he knows all the systems. He sets up Friday night book readings and helps to make these events a success. To replace James, Hannibal would have to take the chance of hiring the right person, take time and spend money training them, and possibly lose that person if they turned out not to be interested.

- James is obviously loyal to Hannibal and wants to remain at the bookstore. He appears to learn quickly and can continue to add to his abilities to support Hannibal's operations.

- If James studies management it could directly benefit Hannibal long-term if James stays and becomes a manager. What he learns at college would directly help Hannibal.

- James loves books and thus there is a great chance he will want to remain in this business indefinitely.

How is reading an important value?

- A value is a continuing belief or way of approaching life. Reading is an important value because it is connected to life-long learning and developing one's capacities and understandings of life and the world in which we live.

- In this case, such a value also supports Hannibal's needs. The value of reading is directly connected to the bookstore business. It will make employees better informed and capable of serving customers and maintaining interest in their work. It also can lead to some creative input by James as to how to better serve the customer and make the business more effective.

Informational Interview Discussion

Discuss how to get information about a selected career field. Below are some suggested questions to ask.

How would you go about getting information about a career?

- Professional associates through Internet and telephone inquiries

- Government statistics through the Internet

- Professional journals in the career field

- Reviewing press articles about the career field

- Informational interview with an expert in the career field

What kind of information is important to get?

- Necessary education and training

- Nature of the work

- Working conditions

- Opportunities in the field

- Important personal strengths to develop for the field

- Advantages of working in the field

- Salary ranges

What other questions would you ask about your selected career field?

CHAPTER 7

Self-Advocacy Presentations

Introduction

Use some examples to introduce the idea that the way someone makes a presentation can greatly affect the other party's response.

- For example, be very demanding of the students in getting their attention immediately and asking for something you need. Then contrast this approach by explaining to the students that you enjoy having them in your class and can you have a moment of their time to discuss something important after class. Ask the students which they are more likely to respond to. Ask the students to explain why.

Ask the students to give you the best excuses they have ever used for not doing their homework. Most likely, these excuses will include the dog ate my homework, someone in my family was sick, I lost my assignment, I had to go to the doctor, etc. All the excuses revolve around a problem **the student** had.

Ask the students how effective they think these excuses are in persuading a teacher that they are serious students and should be given some latitude on missing the homework assignment. Discuss how teachers have heard all these excuses and think of them as just that, excuses. Nothing in these "self-advocacy" presentations helps teachers make a positive assessment of the student.

Now ask the class to think of self-advocacy presentations about a missed homework assignment that would make a favorable impression on a teacher.

Look for presentations that focus on some of the teacher's goals.

Presentations could include the following goals:

- Make up the homework

- Account for the teacher having to take extra time to grade this homework assignment

- Demonstrate that the student is serious about the course work and the missed assignment is not a reflection of the student's attitude

- Demonstrate understanding of the topic or a strong desire to learn about the topic

- Show responsibility for making up the homework, offering to do extra work to demonstrate commitment to learning, etc.

- Focus on the need to learn the subject matter rather than personal problems

- Demonstrate that the student will be successful and a source of pride for the teacher

Role-Play

Select a book that would have some important impact on the students. Tell the students you want them to read the book by the end of the semester. Do not give them a reason. Now ask the class to honestly respond and indicate if they will read the book. Now explain all the reasons the students might enjoy the book and benefit from reading the book. Ask if anyone was persuaded to read the book. This simple example demonstrates the importance of focusing on the other party's needs.

Case #15

Connecting Your Goals with Organizational Goals and Overcoming Rejection

You can make a perfect self-advocacy presentation and the person on the other side might still give you resistance. Learning to handle resistance and remain focused on your presentation and goals are essential skills for success. Learning how to gauge effectiveness is critical to being a successful self-advocate. Finally, a great self-advocate, such as Ebony, never accepts rejection.

Background

Your students have probably experienced a great deal of rejection. Sometimes this experience colors their ability to accurately judge others' reactions to their proposals. The indicators most relied upon are emotional responses from the other party. Someone who smiles and is warm is perceived as accepting their proposals, while someone who may appear stern, serious, and asks many difficult questions is perceived as rejecting their proposals.

It is important to convince students that it is often the stern, hard questioner who is seriously considering the advocacy proposal, and the warm, smiling individual who is just finding a pleasant way to reject the proposal. One strong clue as to how the self-advocacy presentation is going is whether the other party is asking serious, hard questions. Such questions usually indicate genuine engagement in the proposal. The absence of hard questions either indicates complete acceptance of a proposal or more often a total lack of engagement in the presentation.

Students should be encouraged by difficult questions and look at them as an opportunity to connect with the other party and make a convincing presentation. What often seems like rejection of their proposal can be overcome if they can identify the reason behind the rejection or criticism and address this concern in their proposal.

Case Discussion

Review Case #15 and the questions from the student casebook.

Following are some important questions to consider if not already discussed.

Why do people ask hard questions?

- Want to make the best decisions possible
- Are seriously thinking about your proposal
- Want to be convinced about something they didn't understand or resisted

What is a decision-maker's role?

- Make decisions that have consequences in an organization
- Can have great costs or benefits
- Usually under a great amount of pressure

What role does the Human Resource Director or Director of Personnel play in an organization?

Role-Play

Ask students to think of themselves as a student council at a foster care agency asked to screen potential candidates for the position of caseworker (you play the caseworker). In real life, most students are exasperated with having caseworkers who quickly leave their positions, who don't understand young adults, who are too rule-oriented, and who just aren't effective, and this will be demonstrated in the role-play. The students want to make sure a candidate who is highly competent gets hired.

This role-play should get the students asking hard questions and help them better understand that questions are related to the task, not the personality of the perspective candidate.

Assume that Ms. Ward sees Ebony's proposal as an asset for E.L. Jenkins. If so, what does Ms. Ward do or say that indicates support?

- Supports the advice given by Ebony's uncle.

- Respects Ebony's goal.

- Gives Ebony an opportunity to explain her college's ranking.

- Asks Ebony how she can be of help.

- Informs Ebony that there is no "formal" internship program. She could have said they have a policy against all internships. She left the door open.

- Likes the idea of the report and gives Ebony the clue that her objection is the work involved, not the concept.

- Never objects flatly to Ebony's proposal. She only makes sure Ebony understands there are no guarantees.

- Might be testing Ebony to see how far she is willing to go without any commitment. This would test her potential dedication to helping E.L. Jenkins.

Ebony does an excellent job rebuffing Ms. Ward's objections and rejections. She never gets defensive or discouraged. Ebony remains true to her agenda and presents as if Ms. Ward will eventually understand. Ebony controls the agenda and comes across as a very self-assured, assertive winner.

E.L. Jenkins has no formal internship program. Ms. Ward has no time to figure out how to get one started. If Ebony had not designed a solution to this problem, she would most likely not have gotten anywhere. Note that Ebony has a solution and a method for adopting her plan and takes responsibility for executing it, causing no additional work for Ms. Ward.

Do you think it is realistic that Ebony could have come back from such an awful interview as the one she did in Case #2, *Ebony's First Job Interview?*

Why do you think she was able to get another interview?

What things have you messed up and how might you recover?

Do you think people are more interested in how badly you messed up or in your ability to recover from it? Why?

Case #16

Involving Your Allies

Other people familiar with your strengths and accomplishments can help you reach your goals. You have to know how to identify these people, ask them for help, and use their help.

Background

Many students do have access to supporters for helping them enter their desired career, and typically students don't even recognize the importance of having such support. Your students have a big task ahead of them: to develop a supporter network with a minimum of assistance, or even on their own.

From the experience of countless informational interviews, YAC members have observed that our students can develop a network of professionals who will provide some assistance to help them reach their career goals. We need to convince students of the importance of such efforts and sharpen their ability to succeed in gaining the support.

Case Discussion

Review Case #16 and the questions from the student casebook.

Following are some important questions to consider if nto already discussed.

What is the nature of the relationship with an ally, reference, and supporter?

What kinds of people can be allies, references, or supporters?

- Notice that Cheyenne's supporters, allies, and references come from a variety of experiences. It is your responsibility to analyze how your experiences and relationships with each of your allies can be of value.

How do you develop such a relationship?

- Some allies are through long-term experiences, but others can be sought through a short-term relationship such as Ms. Jerome. Informational interviewers may be interested in getting information and developing allies.

Why would someone be interested in being an ally, supporter, or reference?

What does someone need to do to get a person to give them a reference?

- Reference letters can be very useful if they are specific. If the reference knows exactly what needs to be emphasized, the letter can be very important.

- It is a good idea to ask people with whom you work or train whether they would be willing to serve as a reference (someone to call) or write a recommendation letter.

What does Ms. Jerome's suggestion about the summer internship indicate?

- It indicates Ms. Jerome was impressed by Cheyenne and is willing to use her reputation to support Cheyenne's internship application. If Cheyenne did not perform well as an intern, others in the bank might question Ms. Jerome's judgment. Therefore, such a recommendation demonstrates a risk for Ms. Jerome. Even a small risk would not be undertaken without some favorable impressions about Cheyenne's capabilities. Ms. Jerome also knows that if Cheyenne does well, it will reflect well on Ms. Jerome's judgment and benefit her.

How difficult was it for Cheyenne to prepare for and get an informational interview?

- Notice how hard Cheyenne worked to prepare for her interview with Ms. Jerome.

- Getting an informational interview is difficult. Cheyenne worked hard to prepare for this interview and to make a presentation that would interest Ms. Jerome in helping Cheyenne on her path to achieve her long-term goal. Cheyenne researched and got information to sound knowledgeable about her goals and to demonstrate that she was keenly interested in the banking field. Her rejection by six of the recipients of her letters is not a bad percentage. If she tried calling all six again, she might even get one more appointment.

Further Discussion: Mortgages

- People can purchase homes without enough money to pay the full cost. They get a mortgage (loan) that can, in some cases, pay for 90 percent or more. For example, to purchase a $150,000 home or apartment, someone would only need a "down payment" of $8,000–$15,000. The bank pays the rest and allows the homebuyer to pay off this loan (mortgage) over 10 to 30 years. The homebuyer pays "interest" (money) to the bank for getting this mortgage. The homeowner also promises that if they cannot pay, they will allow the bank to sell the home to get their money back.

Case #17

Developing Workable Solutions

*When making a self-advocacy presentation, if you're lucky, you'll get to a point where the other person says, "What do you need from me?" You need to be prepared with **specific** solutions. It is not a good idea to expect the other party to come up with the specific ways to help you, even if they want to be helpful. A skilled self-advocate will develop solutions that will have minimum costs for the other person and may actually result in benefits.*

Background

Young adults often want others to solve their problems. Even when they can articulate their goals, they frequently fail to develop useful means for others to help them. It is important to help your students understand that if they can develop useful solutions that can be employed by the other party, they increase their likelihood of getting support for their goals. Developing useful solutions for the other party also helps them have greater input into the results of self-advocacy.

Case Discussion

Review Case #17 and the questions from the student casebook.

Following are some important questions to consider if not already discussed.

Do you think Gloria Caldwell was rude or inattentive to Tyshanna's request for help? Repeatedly, we need to begin by depersonalizing the process. Context and preparation for self-advocacy are always essential elements.

- Ms. Caldwell has strong reasons to focus on her professional and personal needs, and therefore it is not surprising that in the context of a casual encounter she does not extend herself to support Tyshanna.

Why does Ms. Caldwell act as if college is not that important?

- This is certainly not her personal opinion, having attended college herself and striving for professional achievement. Most likely, she is acting her role within the organization and focused on the immediate goals of maintaining an efficient schedule. Therefore, her expressed attitude about college must be judged within a context.

Is it reasonable that Gloria Caldwell should be knowledgeable about Tyshanna's strengths? If she were, would she be more available to help Tyshanna?

One way to begin the analysis process to prepare a self-advocacy presentation is to begin with Tyshanna's strengths. She has considerable strengths, and many of them are aligned with Cafémeet's needs and goals:

- Her ambition: College and her long-term goals could make her a valuable resource for Cafémeet's future success. Also, her ambition demonstrates an ability to remain focused on goals and to succeed.

- Natural ability with children: Pays off when customers are parents and bring their children. Creating a hospitable atmosphere for children is a strong way of creating customer loyalty.

- Respected by store manager: She performs well and is an asset (valuable resource) for Cafémeet.

- Loyalty to family: An important value that contributes to a high sense of responsibility and being able to deal with difficult situations.

- Financial struggles: Successfully dealing with financial struggles makes her capable of handling budgeting and financial matters in business.

What could be the negative consequences for Cafémeet if Tyshanna were given a more flexible schedule and increase in salary?

- There may be times when Tyshanna might not be present to cover night activities at the store.

- Increased salary could lower profits for store.

- Might create jealousy from other workers who might slack off, especially when Tyshanna was not around.

- Tyshanna's ability to create a hospitable environment for children and their parents might not continue when she was not there.

- Committing herself to college might make Cafémeet fear that Tyshanna would not remain long, and they might hire a new night manager who would commit to a longer tenure.

- Tyshanna's more flexible schedule might cause more scheduling work for Ms. Caldwell.

Why should we consider the impact for Cafémeet?

- Anticipating the consequences for Cafémeet puts Tyshanna in a position to consider ways to diminish the impact or even make them into benefits for Cafémeet.

If Tyshanna wants a raise and a flexible schedule, what could she do to "balance" the costs to Cafémeet?

- Tyshanna could take responsibility for training one night staff person to take over and promise to carefully train and supervise her.

- Tyshanna could demonstrate that college would help her gain new skills that would make her more efficient, offsetting her higher salary. She could also set some goal of either increased efficiency or greater income for the store.

- Tyshanna would have to demonstrate the loyalty of her own night staff and promise to take responsibility that the night work would not slack off.

- Tyshanna could offer to run some specific training for the other staff in creating a hospitable environment for children and parents.

- Tyshanna needs to remind Cafémeet of her ambition to be a regional manager. College is a means for taking on more responsibility at Cafémeet, rather than leaving the establishment.

- Tyshanna could agree to take on the extra work and responsibility for any scheduling changes, instead of leaving that task to Ms. Caldwell.

Creating solutions not only has direct benefits in getting help from others, but it positions the self-advocate as a "problem solver." This increases respect for his or her abilities and makes it easier to advocate the next time. It also has the effect of placing the self-advocate in a higher position in his or her supervisor's mind. For example, if Tyshanna made a successful presentation of her needs and the ways she could help the store provide for those needs, she might be more highly considered for future promotions or more responsible assignments.

Informational Interviews

How can you get career information?

- Guidance counselors

- Professional associations

- Government Labor Department

- Colleges

- Professional journals

- Informational interviews

What is the basic information you could get from these sources?

- Nature of job

- Required training, education, and experience

- Outlook for career field in future

- Geographic areas of concentration

- Range of advancements

- Salary range

Case #18

Developing Strategies

Individuals who are successful find many people who can help them. Finding the right people and getting them interested in helping you is hard work. Yet it's an important step in advocating for yourself. If you identify and reach out to the right people, you can be very successful in saving time and reaching the goals you have established.

Background

Informational interviews (or informational meetings) may significantly help a student get on the path to achieving his or her professional goals. Informational interviews provide valuable information for making plans to achieve long-term goals. They also provide useful contacts for internships, college, and even jobs. Equally important is the elevation of motivation and self-worth that results from the process. While the student's first informational interview is set up for him or her, it is important that the individual also develops the skill to set up informational interviews on his or her own. This will be a powerful self-advocacy skill for the rest of the student's life.

Case Discussion

Review Case #18 and the questions from the student casebook.

Following are some important questions to consider if not already discussed.

Why wasn't Trish discouraged after getting no positive response to her phone requests for an informational interview?

- Her goal is extremely important, and she will not be defeated.

- She may understand that all the people she called are very busy and they need to avoid spending time on new things that seem to have little importance for their work.

- Trish may realize that she hadn't had the opportunity to demonstrate why it might be beneficial to meet with her.

Why would a letter or e-mail be useful after being either ignored or told that there is no time available for an informational interview?

- People often respond to someone who is persistent. Persistence demonstrates seriousness and an ability not to take rejection personally. These are important professional traits.

- Trish may be able to make a better self-advocacy presentation through a short letter or e-mail.

What should Trish think about in planning her letter?

- The reader's needs

- Supporting any of those needs

- Demonstrating her commitment to the profession

- Communicating some of her strengths

In what condition could the professional be in when he or she reads Trish's letter?

- Busy

- Not focused on Trish or her needs

- Not carefully reading the letter

- Resisting any intrusion on his or her time

- Determining how he or she can benefit from such a meeting

An important dynamic is to get the writer to understand that the reader is primarily self-interested in his or her organization and in him- or herself, not in the writer. Breaking through this dynamic is the writer's first goal.

The writer's second goal is to demonstrate how this meeting will benefit the reader as well as the writer. If it just benefits the writer, the reader may not feel able to give the time.

Informational Interview Questions

Talk to students about open versus closed ended questions. Students should ask questions that are specific enough to elicit details.

For example: "Tell me everything about marketing" is much too broad a question. **The following questions are more specific and will result in better information:**

- "What are the most important skills I can have for a marketing job?"

- "I know your marketing work is in the area of engineering services. Is marketing for other areas similar or very different?"

- "What do you like best about your work in marketing?"

- "What is the most difficult part of doing marketing work?"

- "What kind of education is best suited for a marketing career?"

- "Are there specific classes you would recommend I take?"

Case #19

Written Presentations

Sometimes a friend or teacher may help you set up an informational interview. Other times, you have to do it yourself. For an informational interview, you need to talk with someone who has a great deal of responsibility and is usually very busy. It may be hard to set up your appointment over the phone. A letter is a good way to introduce yourself, demonstrate your seriousness, and get the person to focus on your request.

Background

Many students resist communicating in writing. A combination of a limited academic background and inexperience with benefiting from written communication creates this reluctance.

The seminar cannot teach language skills. However, treating written assignments purely as communications assignments and connecting these assignments to relevant issues in students' lives can help students improve their ability to communicate through writing.

You should stress the communication developments in their writing rather than their use or poor use of sentence construction. Students will respond in this context. The issues should be whether students have developed well-thought-out strategies and plans and whether they are effectively communicating their intentions.

Having students write letters requesting an informational interview despite the fact that these interviews have already been arranged is a good way to help students think about the interview's purpose and the expert's motivations.

Case Discussion

Review Case #19 and the questions from the student casebook.

Following are some important questions to consider if not already discussed.

Why didn't Greta begin her letter explaining who she was?

In what context will the potential interviewer most likely read Greta's letter?

- The recipient will most likely read Greta's letter during the business day when he or she is most engaged in work issues. In this context, the reader is not focused on Greta or even interested in who she is. Focusing on the reader or the reader's organization is a better way to gain his or her attention. This beginning paragraph also demonstrates that the writer has some particular knowledge about the Winslow Hotel and is serious.

What is the purpose of the second paragraph in Greta's letter?

Does the second paragraph provide enough information about Greta's strengths?

- The second paragraph gives the reader a sense of the writer's strengths. It demonstrates a commitment and some understanding of the particular demands of hotel management. The reader does not have time to read a résumé, and Greta has done a good job demonstrating enough strengths to communicate her potential.

Greta's letter demonstrates a strategy to get an informational interview. As a self-advocate, Greta knows she has to motivate the reader to respond to her request. From reading her letter, what do you think she believes will be the reader's motivation to give her an informational interview?

- Greta is relying on the idea that the Associate Manager loves and respects her work and enjoys talking about it. Greta believes the reader would be interested in an informational interview if she believed that Greta was serious and had the potential to succeed. If this was true, spending 20 minutes discussing something she loves doing and is knowledgeable about with someone who seriously wants to learn from her would make the reader feel even stronger about her own career choice.

Case #20

Oral Presentations

An informational interview is a meeting with an experienced professional in a career field you have an interest in. The informational interview is not a job interview, but rather an opportunity to get information about a specific job and what education, training, and experience are needed to get such a job. These types of interviews are very important. They can help you reach your goals much faster by learning the best ways to approach and prepare for your chosen career and connecting you with other people who can help you achieve your goals.

People at all levels of success use informational interviews to get ahead in their careers. Even the head of a company who is interested in changing fields or working at a different type of company will set up informational interviews for himself or herself in the same way as someone who is starting out on his or her first job.

Background

The informational interview is a key objective for the semester's work. The experience of engaging in an informational interview with a seasoned professional will be an instrumental factor in your students' success. This interview can be one of the more effective ways to get useful information for analyzing and planning their future goals. We recommend you devote a great deal of time to this process. Encourage students to continue to do informational interviews after their first one this semester.

In judging an interview's success, students often rely on the "niceness" of the professional or the fact that they don't ask difficult questions or raise difficult points. It is important for students to understand that asking difficult questions or raising serious issues indicates that the professional has become interested in the student and has become committed to providing information that will truly help the student make useful plans.

Informational Interview Agenda

To help your students plan for and engage in a useful informational interview, we have designed a model information interview agenda in Appendix D of the student casebook. This agenda has most of the important elements necessary to produce a meeting that will engage the professional and gain useful information.

As you go through Derek's informational interview, have the students recognize as many elements of the agenda as possible. Point out that while the agenda follows a suggested order, this structure frequently changes, especially if the professional becomes fully engaged.

It is important to explain to your students that preparing for the informational interview and designing their agendas will utilize all the skills they learned this semester.

This is a good time to begin reviewing all the previous chapters.

- Making **plans** for how to reach their goals
- Developing a plan based on understanding **how organizations work**
- Identifying **personal strengths** that will demonstrate likelihood of success
- When possible, using advice and support from **mentors and allies**
- Analyzing the other party's **needs** and **depersonalizing** the issues
- Developing a compelling self-advocacy presentation through designing an effective **agenda**
- If relevant, using rules and laws to support their positions

Dynamics of Informational Interview

The information interview's purpose is for a student to gain career information and advice, possibly get a lead on an internship, and establish a resource for future assistance.

There are many reasons why the informational interviewers conduct interviews:

- They recognize they are in a position to help someone starting out.
- They enjoy talking about their work and career.
- They feel useful giving advice.
- They relate to their own experiences starting out and how useful it was when someone helped them.
- They recognize that if they help someone get going in a career, that person may someday be in a position to help them.
- They enjoy meeting new people with fresh perspectives.

Informational Interview Request Letter

Review the letters students wrote to request an informational interview. See if students followed the guidelines in Appendix C of the student casebook.

- Did the first paragraph successfully engage the reader?
- Did the letter present any compelling reasons to help the writer? Did it demonstrate some of the writer's strengths and potential for success?
- Did the letter clearly indicate the writer's career goal?
- Did the writer communicate any benefits to the reader if they agree to the interview?
- Did the writer take the responsibility to follow up?
- Review the student's informational interview agenda.

Preparing for the Informational Interview

Review initial questions and follow-up questions.

Review the presentation of strengths.

Review what students expect the interviewer to ask.

Revisit transitional issues

Suggest to the class that the informational interviewer will be considering the student's potential to succeed.

Can you think of anything that you learned about transitions that would convince the informational interviewer about your commitment to succeed?

One way is to think about what endings you need to make to move on and indicate your willingness or commitment to make such an ending. For example:

- I know that if I go to college and try to get an internship, I have to give up thinking of myself as just a student with few responsibilities.

- I recognize I can no longer keep putting off thinking or planning about my future. From this point on I need to develop a plan and set goals.

Another way is to recognize that doing this informational interview represents that you are, at least partly, in the neutral zone—a gain you might indicate to the interviewer.

- I am committed to finishing high school and going to college. This meeting is very important for me because I need to use this time to really figure out what I am going to do and make plans for reaching my goals. Your advice and information will help me begin to make such decisions.

CHAPTER 8

Rules, Laws, and Rights

Introduction

This chapter is for advanced study. It should only be assigned if you have not fallen behind schedule and if you think the class is up to one more challenging subject. If you skip this chapter, it will have minimum impact on the preparation for the informational interview.

Students often have a misplaced reliance on rules and laws as a guarantee that they will be treated fairly. The challenge is to demonstrate that rules and laws alone are not always proactive and that it takes a successful self-advocate to see that the existing rules and laws are applied in a fair and supportive way. A goal of this chapter is to increase the understanding of how a self-advocate can use existing rules and laws as tools to reach his or her objectives.

Case #21

Using Rules in Advocacy

Rights do not always come from laws made by the government. Rules and rights (sometimes called policies*) can be made by an organization. Policies and rules can be used when you advocate for yourself in an organization. Learning how to use these policies and rules to support your objectives is an important aspect of self-advocacy.*

Background

Young adults often are very keen on their "rights" as well as rules and regulations. They usually have a good instinct for what is fair, and they believe others should abide by the rules. The problems in using rights, rules, regulations, and laws often revolve around differing perspectives of the facts and differing interpretations of the law.

This semester your students have begun to recognize the importance of critical understanding and analysis through working with these cases. Everything has a context and has a different relevance depending upon differing situations. It is important to help the student gain critical understanding and analysis of rules and recognize that rules have meaning in a context.

Many times students have and will find themselves unfairly punished or penalized for something they did. This happens too often and will happen to them in the workplace and out in the community. You will find that students easily relate to this case and empathize with Ashira. Learning how to handle such situations and utilize self-advocacy techniques to reverse the unfair treatment is extremely important.

Case Discussion

Review Case #21 and the questions from the student casebook.

Following are some important questions to consider if not already discussed.

Can rules be contradictory?

- If rules are contradictory, it may be useful to look at the intention behind the rules to resolve the contradiction.

In building a case based around rules, as in all self-advocacy, facts become extremely important. For example, was there coverage in the paint department at the time Ashira went to electrical?

Was other time specifically set aside for Ashira to learn about electrical supplies? Was Ashira provided with a copy of the rules?

Does Ms. Hale have a good reputation as a supervisor?

- Country Depot's mission is also important in developing a self-advocacy presentation.

If Ashira has a good case under the rules, whom should she approach? If she approaches the store manager, can she do it in a way that doesn't antagonize Ms. Hale?

- It's a judgment call. If Ashira tries to depersonalize the situation, she can analyze whether Ms. Hale is honestly doing her job or has some fatal flaw that will make her resist anything Ashira can present. A usual rule is to go first to one's supervisor, in this case, Ms. Hale.

- If, instead, Ashira goes to the store manager, she risks threatening Ms. Hale. If the store manager decides Ashira is correct, then this is an attack on Ms. Hale. If Ashira goes to the store manager, she should try to develop another more important reason than just the incident. For example, she could go to the store manager to talk about her desire to move ahead at Country Depot and express her interest in any training opportunities or ways she can advance her position. If the store manager is receptive, Ashira could in passing mention the incident but not put the manager in the position of overruling Ms. Hale. For example, Ashira could say, "Just wanted you to know Ms. Hale was very upset that I was away from my station and talking to Latoya in electrical. I had to show a customer where electrical was, but while I was there, I wanted to learn more about electrical. Next time I'll do it when I am not supposed to be covering the paint area. I made a mistake."

- This explanation places no blame on Ms. Hale for being unfair and places all the responsibility on Ashira. However, it does demonstrate an important and work-related reason why she had not returned to the paint department. In the store manager's mind, Ashira looks like someone responsible and committed to moving ahead. If the store manager is experienced, he or she may take care of the disciplinary notice without any further self-advocacy.

Is it possible to turn this situation into a positive for Ashira?

If she talks with Ms. Hale about rescinding the notification, can she also advocate for other goals? Can she take a meeting about a problem and turn it into a meeting about something that would benefit Country Depot and Ms. Hale?

Place yourself in Ms. Hale's position. Why do you think Ms. Hale would act the way she did? Why would she

- Stop and notice Ashira away from her station?

- Notify Ashira through written notice rather than personally?

- Not inform Ashira of any rights she has to present an explanation?

In your analysis of Ms. Hale's actions, look for the non-personal reasons.

- Ms. Hale is too busy and overwhelmed with all her responsibilities to take time to personally solve every problem.

- Ms. Hale's management style is to adhere strictly to what she perceives as the rules.

- Ms. Hale is confident that a well-motivated worker will take initiative to correct a misjudgment she made.

This process will actually help a self-advocate develop useful solutions for resolving the present problem.

Case #22

Applying Rules, Laws, and Rights in Self-Advocacy Presentations

Knowledge of the law can be useful in self-advocacy. Laws can be thought of as agreed-upon rules that will be respected for resolving disputes. In most cases, knowing the laws and using your understanding of the laws will help to resolve a dispute without having to go to court.

Example of Laws Supporting Jill

- There are state laws that protect consumers when they purchase a new product. Such laws provide that a new product is expected to work as designed even if there is no written guarantee.

- There are also laws that require merchants to fairly represent (accurately describe) what they sell.

- In many cities, there are laws that require landlords to paint apartments for new tenants and to keep the appliances in working order.

- Knowing these laws make most merchants (people who sell things, retailers), landlords, customers, and tenants capable of resolving problems without going to court.

Background

When confronted with common, real-life experiences, students need to prepare to protect their rights and their finite resources. They will experience a wide range of adverse situations where they will need to rely quickly on their self-advocacy skills. The following are a range of such situations they might face. Knowing the law and then how to self-advocate will greatly help them protect themselves and, in some cases, recover their losses.

Case Discussion

Review Case #22 and the questions from the student casebook.

Following are some important questions to consider if not already discussed.

In every situation described where Jill is taken advantage of, it is clear there is something wrong and unfair. How can she find out whether there is an actual legal violation?

- She should begin by calling the consumer affairs department or the state attorney general's office. They can usually tell you the law and help suggest ways to correct the situation or possibly give direct help. This type of research is strong self-advocacy.

Facts and analysis are important. What are the important facts relevant to helping Jill solve the problems connected with her purchase and the apartment?

- The bureau was represented as an "antique from 1911." Yet it was put together with staples and tape not available in 1911. Clearly there was a misrepresentation.

- In Jill's apartment, the stove does not work. The landlord promised to paint and fix the stove. The law also requires the landlord to fix the stove and paint the rest of the apartment.

- She purchased a new television set that is obviously used and has defective sound. If an appliance is represented as new, it must be new. If the appliance is new and is defective, either the store or manufacturer is responsible for fixing the appliance.

- The bed is the most difficult problem because it was purchased as used and not represented as anything. The broken leg may not be the store's fault. However, they may have a moral or business responsibility to fix the leg.

- Jill must also analyze the problem with the fraudulent credit account. Just removing the bill may not correct her credit rating. She may have to do more self-advocacy to fix that problem.

Perhaps the store was unaware of the condition of the TV and wants to do the right thing. In many businesses, customer satisfaction is critically important. This can be a tool for the self-advocate. If Jill has a positive experience getting the TV replaced, she will recommend that store to her friends. If not, she can hurt the store's reputation. The point is that she must begin the advocacy process by depersonalizing the problem and assuming that everyone wants to do the right thing. If this is not true, she can become a much more assertive advocate.

Most people who have passions can turn them into professional goals. Jill's passion for the environment can turn into a well-paying job in an area she enjoys.

Further Discussion

- Most students have inadequate information about college. This fact undermines their ability to make an effective long-term career plan. Whenever possible, try to help students understand college education and the specific role it plays in preparing them to achieve successful independence and career goals. A master's degree is an advanced degree after four years of college. It is usually in a specific area and takes two to three years to complete. In many masters programs, students can have some work-study or part-time job in the field they are studying.

- Renting an apartment usually requires a security deposit for possible damage to the apartment. It usually consists of one month of rent. Usually a tenant cannot just stop paying rent if the landlord does not comply with his or her obligations. Instead, they can go to housing court and perhaps pay into an escrow (held by court) account until the landlord complies.

Informational Interview

Next week, students should be prepared to role-play their informational interviews. It is preferable to seek an outside guest to role-play the different experts the students have selected for their interviews. You can do the role-play yourself, but adding an outside person adds to the feeling of what it will be like when they do the actual interview.

Inform students they should be prepared next week with their final agenda and that each student will get 10 minutes to conduct a practice interview, followed by feedback from the class. Explain that this practice role-play is essential because it will help them prepare and strengthen their actual presentations. Having an opportunity to practice will help them see which areas need strengthening and will make them much more comfortable during the actual interview.

Role-Play of Informational Interview

This class is devoted totally to the role-play of the informational interview. Have each student present to the class who his or her informational interviewer will be (profession, position, and any other information the student has), and then have the student and "interviewer" start the role-play at the introduction. For the class's benefit, you or whoever does the role-play for the experts should try to cover a range of possible experts to give the class a comprehensive view of what they can expect. For example, in one interview you might play someone who seems a bit distracted and serious but asks hard and engaging questions. Another type might be confused about the interview's purpose. Another might be very sociable and want to discuss all sorts of subjects that are not directly related to the interview's purpose. Some interviewers may be very encouraging and others might be less than encouraging.

By playing the range of personalities, students can learn how to adjust their presentations and how to develop their ability to focus on positive rather than negative feedback.

After each role-play, have the class give the student feedback. Encourage positive as well as critical feedback and encourage each student to give alternative approaches. Help students go beyond the interviewer's personality type to harvest the real value of the interview. When students act surprised at the different personality types, help them understand that having rigid expectations will only hinder their performance.

Post-Interview Discussion

The feedback from the informational interview is critical for the learning process. Hearing from each student what he or she learned and experienced will help every member of the group gain solid insight into the professional world.

Many students will be enthusiastic about the response and encouragement they received during the informational interview. Help them present some of the specific career information they received from their interviews.

Ask students what their next steps will be and encourage them to start making a plan.

Try to highlight commonalities from the interviews. For example, all interviewees probably stressed higher education, voiced past setbacks and failures, explained the role of persistence and motivation in success, and talked to each student with respect as a future colleague. Reinforce their achievement of conducting the interview on their own and that success was totally based on their talent and ability to present themselves.

Use the feedback from the informational interview as a means of providing useful feedback to your students, but in your own words, rather than the interviewees. It is best to provide feedback using the Socratic Method.

Final Evaluation

The final evaluation can be found at www.jost.com/K1653/appendices.pdf. Explain to the students that they will have 45 minutes to complete the evaluation.

Student Application

On Your Own as a Young Adult: Self-Advocacy Seminar is designed for students who want to take control of their future and make sure they will succeed when they become independent. Students who want to learn how to advocate for themselves and find the best way to plan for their futures will find this seminar very helpful.

Students that take the seminar go on individual informational interviews where they meet with a professional in their chosen career field. These informational interviews help students begin to plan their future career and make decisions that will promote success. Whether you want to be a pastry chef, marine biologist, teacher, graphic artist, computer professional, health care professional, legal professional, plumber, teacher, or whatever, this seminar will help you develop a usable plan to get where you want to go.

Only students willing to engage in the seminar work, support others in the class, and make a commitment to help themselves are admitted into the seminar. If you are interested, please answer the following questions.

1. What career would you like to work in?

   _____

   _____

2. In one or two sentences, describe why you are interested in the career goal you selected.

   _____

   _____

   _____

   _____

   _____

3. Describe some your strengths (things you are good at).

   _____

   _____

   _____

   _____

   _____

4. Would you describe yourself as someone who is willing to work at something to achieve a long-term goal? Explain.

_____

_____

_____

_____

_____

_____

_____

_____

_____

5. What are the two most important things you need to do to prepare for complete independence? Describe how you will accomplish these goals.

_____

_____

_____

_____

_____

_____

_____

_____

_____

Name_____ Date_____

Date of Birth_____

Address_____

City_____

Phone Number_____

E-mail Address_____

Requirements Contract

Welcome to the *On Your Own as a Young Adult: Self-Advocacy Seminar*. After you complete the seminar, you will join a select group of graduates who have learned how to achieve their long-term goals through self-advocacy.

Schedule of Class Meetings:

_____

_____

_____

_____

_____

Location:

_____

_____

_____

_____

_____

Please read the following contract and make sure you understand everything before you sign it. Ask a supportive staff member or a family member to read and sign this contract.

If you complete the seminar, you will

- Learn how to reach your personal goals through self-advocacy.

    You will gain skills and experience in

    - Establishing long- and short-term goals

    - Presenting your strengths

    - Developing supporters and allies

    - Understanding the needs of the other party

    - Using your experiences in the system to your advantage

    - Planning agendas

    - Problem analysis

- Writing self-advocacy letters

- Making presentations

- Conducting informational interviews

- Learn and improve self-advocacy skills to reach your goals.

- Learn to conduct an informational interview with an expert to gather information and make contacts for achieving your long-term career goals.

- Receive a Certificate of Self-Advocacy Competency. You may also request a recommendation letter that you can use for applying to college or getting a job.

- Be eligible to become a Youth Advocate Workshop Peer Leader and train to make public presentations about self-advocacy to other youth in the system.

- Be better prepared to take college-level courses.

- Make new and important friendships with other students.

The Seminar

The seminar will consist of class once per week. Through discussion, instruction, and your participation, you will learn how to advocate for yourself. The seminar is designed for students who want to succeed in their future lives.

Each week you will be given written assignments. Don't worry! You can get help when you need it. Throughout the seminar, you will also learn how to conduct an informational interview.

The Informational Interview

The informational interview is the major project for the semester's work. In this interview, you will gain an opportunity to practice the self-advocacy skills you learned during the semester. You will also have the opportunity to gain valuable information about your intended career and methods to reach your goals in the field. Your informational interview will be of great importance to achieving your long-term goals.

You will select a career field as your long-term goal. During the semester, an informational interview will be set up for you with a high-level, experienced professional in the career field you have selected. A great deal of time and effort is devoted to setting up these interviews and it is expected that each student will make a major effort to make these interviews successful.

Requirements for Completing Advocacy Seminar

1. **Time Requirements**

   - You must attend all seminar sessions.

   - The seminar sessions will be on _____.

- You must arrive **on time** and remain through the entire session.

- You must work an additional ＿＿＿＿＿ hours a week on homework.

- You may miss **only** one seminar session for illness or emergency.

  (A missed day consists of any time you either miss a seminar session or are late to a session.) You are required to make up the missed work.

- You will need to devote extra time to prepare for your informational interview.

2. Your Homework

- There will be written homework for every week. You must complete all assignments on time.

- Homework will be evaluated and given a grade. If homework is late, your grade will be lowered.

- If you have difficulty completing the homework, it is your responsibility to get help from your facilitator or from a supportive staff member.

3. Your Participation

- You must show that you are willing to contribute to group discussions in a constructive manner. You need to demonstrate support for other students by respecting their opinions and by allowing others to be heard.

- You must respect the facilitator when he or she asks you to stop talking or stop behavior that distracts the facilitator or the other group members. Disruptive members will be given a warning. If the disruptive behavior continues after the warning, that member will be asked to withdraw from the seminar.

4. Group Support

- The seminar requires a supportive environment. You are required to assist every student in the seminar by demonstrating respect and contributing ideas that will help others master their own self-advocacy objectives. Each student will have different strengths and weaknesses. You must make an effort to gain from the strengths of others and help others find ways to strengthen weaknesses related to learning self-advocacy.

5. Evaluations and Exams

- You will be required to take an evaluation test before and after the seminar. You must satisfactorily pass the final evaluation given at the seminar's completion. If you have difficulty taking tests, you may take this test several times until you pass.

6. Your Final Project

- You must identify a long-term career goal. In addition, you must prepare for and engage in an informational interview with an expert in your selected career.

I, _____, have read and understand the rules for the self-advocacy seminar. I understand that the *On Your Own as a Young Adult: Self-Advocacy Seminar* is extremely important for my future success and will make every effort to learn and practice self-advocacy skills. I also understand that acceptance into this seminar requires a full commitment of time and effort as outlined above.

_____   _____
Student's Signature   Date

_____   _____
Facilitator's Signature   Date

Student Information   **Support Person Information**

_____   _____
Intended Career Field   Support Person (Print Name)

_____   _____
Date of Birth   Support Person (Signature)

_____   _____
Address   Relationship to Student

_____   _____
City, State, ZIP   Phone Number

_____
Phone Number(s)

_____
E-mail Address

On Your Own as a Young Adult Video

Background

Informational interviews may significantly help a student get on the path to achieving his or her professional goals. These "informational interviews" provide valuable information for making plans to achieve long-term goals. They also provide useful contacts for internships, college, and even jobs. Equally important is the elevation of motivation and self-worth that results from the process. While the student's first informational interview is set up for him or her, it is important that the individual also develops the skill to set up informational interviews on his or her own. This will be a powerful self-advocacy skill for the rest of the student's life.

Ask the class to think of other information gathering questions. Students will be able to use many of these questions for developing their own individual agendas.

Show the video *On Your Own as a Young Adult*.

Discussion

Below are suggested questions to start a discussion about the video.

Does it appear that Nelson is any less capable than Sashine? Why?

- Nelson has ambition, appears to be well-spoken, and shows resilience in continuing to look for work even when everything seems to be against him. He definitely appears to be highly capable.

If they both have great capabilities, why is Nelson still having a hard time finding a decent job?

- Nelson even says how no one explained to him what to do. The biggest difference is that Nelson has little idea how to plan to reach his long-term goals while Sashine has information and is pursuing a plan to reach her goal.

If Nelson did not have as much information and support to pursue his professional goals, could he have done anything about it when he was still in high school?

- Nelson unfortunately assumed someone would help him learn what he had to do. He waited until it was too late. Sashine took responsibility while she was still in high school and foster care to learn what she had to know to reach her goals.

Sashine took a big step to learn more about reaching her goal by going on the informational interview.

- If Nelson had done a few informational interviews with attorneys, perhaps he could have learned what he would have to do to prepare for his future and would have been more motivated to do it.

What do you think were the most important benefits of Sashine's interview?

- Learning from a professional that she has the ability to succeed in her chosen career field motivated Sashine to seriously pursue all the steps necessary to reach her goals.

- Learning about the nature and importance of college.

- Discovering what she would do in college.

- Understanding how her strengths would benefit her in the profession.

- Establishing a contact in the graphic arts field will help Sashine in the future as a resource to answer other questions.

Why do you think the informational interviewer wanted to help Sashine?

- He appreciated Sashine's strengths and motivation, and he realized Sashine was determined and had the ability to succeed. Sashine was well-prepared and took the interview seriously, demonstrating respect for the informational interviewer.

Do you think her background in foster care will make it impossible for Sashine to succeed? Why?

- No. Her struggles may help her in this high-pressure field. Sashine focused on her strengths and the informational interviewer's reaction to her past struggles in foster care was positive and seen as strength.

The video doesn't show how Sashine dealt with all the challenges of going to college. What do you think those challenges were and how do you think Sashine dealt with them?

- She needed to budget her expenses by figuring out how much she would need to cover these expenses and the source of this money. She probably had to get financial aid for college and perhaps take out available loans. Most likely she would still have a part-time job. This is a lot to manage and she probably had to meet with and get advice and information from financial aid counselors, job placement departments at her college, etc.

Did it appear that Sashine used an agenda? Why did she use the agenda?

- Yes. She was very nervous, and it was clear in the video that she had an agenda to remember everything she wanted to cover and she took notes. The agenda also helped to keep the interview focused and impressed the informational interviewer with her seriousness and preparation.

Was Sashine well-prepared for the informational interview? How do you know?

- Yes. She had an agenda. She appeared to cover everything she needed, and she was highly successful in engaging the informational interviewer's help.